MOVEMENT AND MAKING DECISIONS

The Body-Mind Connection in the Workplace

Carol-Lynne Moore

Dance & Movement Press™

New York

Published in 2005 by Rosen Book Works, Inc.

Exclusively distributed by The Rosen Publishing Group, Inc., New York

Book design by Chris Logan and Jennifer Crilly

For more information regarding Dance & Movement Press, contact The Rosen Publishing Group, Inc., 29 East 21st Street, New York, NY 10010, or call 1-800-237-9932. Visit our Web site at http://www.rosenpublishing.com.

Cover (top) © Walter Hodges/Getty Images, (bottom) © Archive Holdings Inc/Getty Images; p. 7 Photographic History Collection, National Museum of American History, Smithsonian Institution, 2004-47489; pp. 8, 9 Musée Marey, Beaune, France; p. 15 Smithsonian Institution, National Museum of American History, 83-3180; pp. 21 (left and right) 23, 37, 39 from the Rudolf Laban Archive, National Resource Centre for Dance. Used with permission.

"Framework" charts on pp. 43, 49, and 80 used with permission © Warren Lamb.

Library of Congress Cataloging-in-Publication Data

Moore, Carol-Lynne.
    Movement and making decisions : the body-mind connection in the workplace/ by Carol-Lynne Moore.— 1st ed.
    p. cm. — (Contemporary discourse on movement and dance)
    Includes bibliographical references and index.
    ISBN 1-59791-000-7 (lib. bdg.)
    1. Movement, Psychology of. 2. Mind and body. 3. Work—Psychological aspects. I. Title. II. Series.

BF295.M63 2005
158.7—dc22
                                        2004023604

CONTENTS

Acknowledgments

Behind every book lie the efforts of many. In particular, I would like to thank Nancy Allison of Rosen Publishing, whose vision brought this series into being and whose intelligent guidance and support were indispensable. The staff at the National Resource Centre for Dance in England provided much aid and assistance. A special thanks to Archive and Research Officer Chris Jones, who helped me penetrate a mass of Laban Lawrence Industrial Rhythm material expeditiously. The pianist Ronald Meachen, whose untimely demise preceded the publication of this book, was very generous in reminiscing with me about his movement work with Warren Lamb in the late 1950s. Frank McKone was equally generous in sharing his 25 years of experience using Movement Pattern Analysis as a corporate client.

I could never have done any of the research and writing without the support of my family. Many thanks to the "Three K's"—Kaoru, Keita, and Kiyomi—for being the lights of my life.

Finally, I would like to acknowledge Warren Lamb, friend and mentor for many years. Working on this book has provided more insight into the genuinely creative contribution he has made to understanding patterns of movement and their behavioral significance in the workplace.

INTRODUCTION

Once upon a time, all economies were small economies. Mass production had not been invented. There were no mechanized assembly lines or high-speed computers to assist human efforts. Individually and collectively, hard physical labor was necessary to secure a livelihood. Craft, too, was visceral, and depended upon the adept coordination of mind, hand, and limb. Prior to the Industrial Revolution, human movement was the crucial ingredient in skilled as well as unskilled labor. The body-mind connection in the workplace was quite palpable, for it took intelligent physical action to produce sustenance and goods.

However, the necessity for hard physical labor has diminished over the last 250 years as increasingly sophisticated and powerful machines have taken over jobs once done by men and women. In industrialized economies today, full-body exertion in the workplace is the exception, not the rule. Yet as demands on the muscles have decreased, other demands on the worker have increased. The Information Revolution with its abundant, often overwhelming, quantity of information has made decision making easier for some people and more stressful for many others. It has also made reality more virtual, creating a separation between body and mind in the workplace.

Yet no matter how cerebral or sedentary the job, the worker cannot escape from the body. As sociologist Bryan Turner observes, "The body is at once the most solid, the most elusive, illusory, concrete, metaphorical, ever present and ever distant thing."[1] Like it or not, people are constrained to labor by means of this paradoxical "thing," for the body remains the source of all being and doing.

Indeed, bodily action is significant; it matters. This is so because what we do changes the world, and it also changes us. Individual character is revealed, perhaps even established, by physical actions performed again and again. Habits of thought are difficult to discern. But habitual ways of moving are readily perceived. It is by means of these patterns of embodied action that we recognize and distinguish among those with whom we live and work.

An example drawn from Japanese history clearly illustrates how patterns of action become keys to character. In the war-torn period (1534–1615) leading up to the unification of Japan, there were three remarkable military leaders: Nobunaga, Hideyoshi, and Ieyasu. Each man was instrumental in moving the nation toward consolidation although, as leaders, each employed very different decision-making strategies. Nobunaga was known for his rash decisiveness; Hideyoshi for his clever determination; and Ieyasu for his ability to bide his time until the right moment to strike. As the novelist Eiji Yoshikawa notes, the divergent philosophies of these three great figures "have long been recalled by the Japanese in a verse known to every school-child."[2] In this verse, the fragmented Japan is compared to a nightingale that won't sing. How would each man handle such a bird?

Nobunaga answers, 'Kill it!'

Hideyoshi answers, 'Make it want to sing.'

Ieyasu answers, 'Wait.'[3]

It was Ieyasu who finally suppressed his enemies, unifying the nation and becoming the great shogun. His reputation for patience was not based upon a single act, but upon a pattern of actions that were decisively influential and writ large in the history of Japan.

Like Ieyasu, every person's characteristic way of making decisions is made legible in his or her pattern of action. And because the body is the seat of all action, character may be read in a person's pattern of movement. In examining the relationship between movement and making decisions, this book focuses on how actions are embodied in the workplace. This is done in the context of recounting the role of movement study in the industrial redesigning of human labor. This redesign was initially carried forward by the time and motion experts, who were concerned with enhancing the efficiency of work movement and increasing productivity. Over time, concerns with the reduction of fatigue, with the selection and placement of workers, and with job satisfaction became more salient. New approaches to movement study were developed to handle these needs, although the focus remained on blue collar occupations in which labor was primarily physical.

A quantum leap occurred, however, when the scope of consideration expanded beyond the study of blue collar labor to the analysis of clerical and managerial functions. White collar jobs presumably involved mental rather than physical effort. And yet, a body-mind connection was inescapably detected, demonstrating that patterns in body movement were related to patterns in decision making integral to clerical and managerial job functions.

This conceptual leap occurred over 60 years ago. Since that time, the discipline of movement analysis has been applied to create profiles of decision-making style based upon patterns of embodied action. These profiles have been used in the selection, placement, and career guidance of managers, as well as in the development of managerial talent and the formation of executive teams. As a consequence, the body-mind connection in the workplace is palpable once again. How the art and science of work study unfold the elusive nature of movement to reveal human character is the story told in the following pages.

Endnotes

1. Bryan S. Turner, *The Body and Society* (New York: Basil Blackwell, 1984), 8.

2. Eiji Yoshikawa, *Taiko* (Tokyo: Kodansha International, 1992), Note to Reader.

3. Ibid.

1 THE DISSECTION OF TIME AND MOTION

Revolution!

The late nineteenth and early twentieth centuries witnessed vast changes in the way that work was done. The second industrial revolution—the electrification of the factory—harnessed a new source of power for the mechanization of labor. The development of the moving assembly line and the concept of standardized parts, improvements pioneered by Henry Ford in the manufacture of automobiles, cut costs and speeded production. The invention of the electrical lightbulb by Ford's friend Thomas Alva Edison provided a steady and safe source of illumination that made it possible for factories to be operated around the clock. For fin de siècle industrialists and inventors, there appeared to be a limitless horizon of increasing productivity and profitability. For the common man, the quality of life was altered and improved to such an extent that "people who lived in 1750 would not have recognized the world of 1914."[1]

In order to understand the profundity of these changes, it is necessary to describe briefly the nature of labor prior to the waves of industrialization that gradually swept over Europe and the United States. In the preindustrial period, before the introduction of steam power in the 1750s, human beings, animals, wind, and running water were the only sources of energy for work. These sources were limited by nature in terms of strength, endurance, location, and dependability. Hard physical labor was needed and this was concentrated on agricultural production. Consequently, the majority of people lived in the countryside, on farms or in small villages. Manufacturing was small in scale and done in homes or local workshops. There was little specialization. Agriculture employed the whole family, for men, women, and children were all needed to work the farm. In the skilled trades as well, artisans were responsible for producing an entire product from beginning to end.[2] In general, occupations were hereditary and traditional; one did what one's parents had done. Or if one learned a skilled trade, this was done through

4

an apprenticeship system in which the craft knowledge of the master was passed down, guaranteeing a continuity in working methods. Thus, preindustrial economies were bound by tradition, constrained by natural limits, and small in scale.

As historians Peter Stearns and John Hinshaw point out, the Industrial Revolution altered this framework.[3] It brought about fundamental changes in the way people worked, where they lived, and the potential economic surplus available. Ramifications of these changes extended not only into systems of production and exchange, but also into habits of thought and relations between men and women, workers and employers, governments and citizens. Industrialization introduced economic growth, innovation, and means of production that were not subject to the limits of nature, and it did so on a scale never before imagined.

This "revolution" was a gradual process, affecting some industries and some countries more than others. However, by the 1880s the following trends were evident throughout western Europe.[4] Agriculture was becoming mechanized, and home manufacturing had virtually disappeared. Population distribution had shifted, for the majority of people now needed to live in towns and cities to find work. Machine use steadily increased, as steam, electricity, and the new internal combustion motors provided power surpassing that of man, animal, wind, and water. Everything grew bigger. Occupations were no longer hereditary or traditional. Some jobs disappeared while new vocations became available for men, women, and children, provoking vast social change and unrest. Governments were forced to abandon the laissez faire policies of the early industrial period and to begin enacting legislation that regulated work conditions, pay, and hours. At the same time, industry itself became more concerned with the conscious management of workers, redefining work discipline, introducing more specialization and division of labor, and increasing the pace and coordination of work units.

This was indeed a new world where, to paraphrase Bishop Heber, every prospect was pleasing and only man was vile. For indeed, the one flaw in this heaven of unlimited productivity was the human one. The factory worker could not labor indefinitely, at ever-increasing rates of speed. He or she grew tired, slowed down, made mistakes, or fell prey to injury and discontent. While parts might be standardized, approaches to job function were not yet regulated. In many industries still influenced by preindustrial craft practices, workers brought their own tools and went about the job in individual ways, with consequent differences in efficiency and output.

Clearly, the human element in industrial production needed retooling. And so, just about 120 years ago, the science of work study was born. This chapter examines the history of this new science. It illustrates how relationships between time, human movement, and productivity were dissected. And it reveals how human labor was redesigned by an English photographer, a French physiologist, and a couple of American engineers. This is not an irrelevant chronicle, for the individuals described here literally reconceived the human body and reconstructed the nature of work. Their innovations are still in use today and influence the labors of millions of people, whether they work on the factory floor or in the executive suite.

Instantaneous Photography and the Dissection of Movement

This chronicle begins, curiously enough, with a bet. Leland Stanford, the American railroad magnate, had wagered a friend that a horse's legs all leave the ground during a trot. Stanford hired the English photographer Eadweard Muybridge to provide photographic confirmation. In 1872 Muybridge obtained the world's first instantaneous photographs of a trotting horse, showing all four legs off the ground. The photographs were published in American, English, and French scientific publications, where they created a sensation. Aspects of animal movement that had never been seen before suddenly became visible through the medium of photography.

Muybridge's revolutionary photographic technique involved setting up a battery of cameras by the side of a track along which the subject was moving. These cameras, which were set off electrically at variable intervals, captured snapshots of various phases of the activity with a precision never before achieved. After his initial success with the horse, Muybridge extended his study to other types of animal motion and to the study of human movement. Working at the University of Pennsylvania, Muybridge produced about 20,000 instantaneous photographs between 1872 and 1885. These were published in 1887 in portfolio form and later in smaller, popular editions.

Artists were among the most avid followers of Muybridge's work. There were those, such as the French painter Ernest Meissonier and the American artist Charles Russell, who wholeheartedly accepted photographic evidence

Muybridge applied his instantaneous technique to capture simple work actions, such as this man planing wood. While Muybridge expected his photographs to be widely used by artists, the images proved to be curiously static. The illusion of movement disappeared, and what remained was a series of frozen poses.

and altered their representations accordingly. Other artists, such as Edgar Degas and Auguste Rodin, were attracted to the naturalism of Muybridge's work without becoming slavish imitators of the photographic image. Above all, Muybridge's work challenged conventional representations of movement and provoked critical discussion within the artistic community.[5] For example, the fact that instantaneous photos revealed unseen aspects of rapid motion was considered a liability by some artists, who questioned the validity of depicting a pose or attitude that could not be perceived in normal life. Moreover, the snapshots "produced a curiously static impression."[6] By isolating one moment from the natural flow of actions, the instantaneous photos tended, ironically, to destroy the impression of movement.

Reaction in the scientific community was perhaps more uniformly positive. For the physiologists and psychophysicists who were concerned with movement and bodily function, Muybridge's work demonstrated that "photography could become an instrument of exceptional precision for recording."[7] The decomposition of a continuous process of motion into discrete poses that appeared quite static was not a concern to scientists. What was of concern was the temporal precision of the sequence of snapshots. The rigor of Muybridge's technique was questioned, and the French physiologist Etienne-Jules Marey set out to solve this problem. Chronophotography was the result.

Temporal Graphs of Motion

Marey (1830–1904) was a distinguished physiologist known for his studies of blood circulation and animal and human locomotion. Marey had already invented a number of mechanical devices to record physiological functions when he encountered Muybridge's photos of the horse in 1878. These snapshots opened his eyes to the possibilities of photography. However, his disappointment with the "non-sequential snapshots of birds in flight produced by Muybridge in 1881," alerted Marey to a technical flaw—Muybridge did not keep the temporal interval between snapshots equal.[8] As a consequence, Muybridge's "images were spatially distinct but temporally blurred."[9]

These difficulties spurred Marey to develop his own device, a photographic gun, in 1882. This instrument could record a dozen images in a second, allowing the flight of a bird to be traced. But the images were fuzzy. Marey went on to experiment with a single camera that superimposed sequential images onto a single plate. By moving the camera in synchrony with the action being photographed, Marey was able to keep the time between exposures roughly equivalent. Marey christened his invention "chronophotography" and set about applying it to the study of animal and human motion. For example, he "clothed men in black, painted white lines along their arms and legs, and had them run or walk against a black background while moving exposures were made on the same plate."[10] The result was a linear graph of the movement of the arms and legs that reduced the general shape of the subject to "moving lines and dots."[11] In this way, Marey managed "to isolate scientifically useful information" with an almost

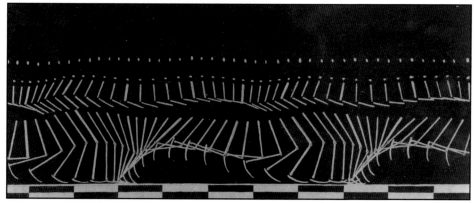

Marey's chronophotograph of a man running converts the human figure into a series of angular lines, facilitating mechanical analysis of arm and leg movements.

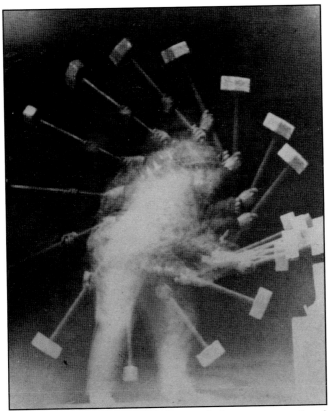

Intermediate positions in the swinging of a hammer are captured in Fremont's chronophotograph of a forger at work.

mathematical accuracy.[12] At the time, his studies "entirely renewed the understanding of the mechanical functions performed by human muscles and bones."[13]

According to historian Anson Rabinbach, "The first application of chronophotography to the study of physical labor was undertaken in Marey's laboratory in 1894."[14] The chronophotographs of forgers hammering red-hot iron were taken by Charles Fremont, an engineer investigating optimum work performance in relation to specific tools. Cinematography, invented the year after Fremont's photos were taken, gradually replaced photography in laboratory research. Nevertheless, instantaneous photographs and chronophotography had demonstrated that continuous flows of activity could be broken into discrete parts for purposes of scientific study. This analytical decompositon of movement was destined to find an even wider application in the practical science of work study, as more engineers turned their attention to human factors in industry.

Scientific Management

The American engineer Frederick Winslow Taylor (1856–1915) was a prime mover in the practical study of work. After abandoning the study of law due to vision problems, Taylor was apprenticed to learn the trades of pattern maker and machinist. He worked his way up in the steel industry, from machine shop laborer to foreman and, eventually, after earning a degree in mechanical engineering, to chief engineer. Taylor revealed a talent for mechanical invention, patenting over forty devices. But his most famous brainchild was "Scientific Management," a radical new approach to work study.

The "science" consisted of careful observation, analysis, and quantification of factory operations. The goal was to increase productivity by eliminating wasted time and motion. As Rabinbach describes, Scientific Management included

> (1) the division of all shop-floor tasks into their fundamental parts; (2) the analysis and design of each task to achieve maximum efficiency and ease of imitation; (3) the redesign of tools and machines as standardized models; (4) the linking of wages to output; and (5) rational coordination and administration of production.[15]

Taylor's approach was revolutionary. As intellectual historian Gerhard Masur notes, the first 100 years of the Industrial Revolution "had proceeded by trial and error."[16] Management as such was in the hands of the shop foremen, who based their approach on experience rather than objective scientific method. By enlisting the expertise of engineers in redesigning work processes, Taylor transformed both labor and management simultaneously. As Taylor himself testified to a committee of the United States Congress in 1912,

> Scientific management is not any efficiency device. . . . It is not a new system of figuring costs . . . it is not holding a stop watch on a man and writing things down about it; it is not time study; it is not motion study . . . in essence, scientific management involves a complete revolution on the part of the working man . . . and it involves the equally complete mental revolution on the part of those on the management's side.[17]

It is interesting to trace the way Taylor went about this revolutionary process. One classic case was his study of shoveling coal at the Bethlehem Steel Company. When Taylor was called in as a consultant, the coal yard was quite large, 1 to 2 miles long and a quarter mile wide. Many varieties of coal and coke were shoveled by 400 to 600 workers, who labored in groups of 25 to 100 under the supervision of various foremen. Taylor's goal was to ascertain the "shovel load at which a first-class shoveler will do his biggest day's work."[18] This optimum load was to be determined by a controlled experiment.

As Taylor recounted, they called in a number of men and from this group chose two first-class shovelers. These men were then addressed as follows:

"See here, Pat and Mike, you fellows understand your job all right; both of you fellows are first-class men; you know what we think of you; you are all right now; but we want to pay you fellows double wages. We are going to ask you to do a lot of damn fool things, and when you are doing them there is going to be someone out alongside of you all the time, a young chap with a piece of paper and a stop watch and pencil, and all day long he will tell you to do these fool things, and he will be writing down what you are doing and snapping the watch on you and all that sort of business. Now, we just want to know whether you fellows want to go into that bargain or not?"[19]

The two shovelers agreed and were set to work on the same task in separate parts of the yard, while two engineers studied the operation. Then various experiments with shovel redesign were undertaken. The shovel was made smaller, so that each shovelful of coal weighed less. Alternatively, the shovel was made larger, so that the load was increased. Speed of shoveling and output were measured by the observing engineers, until the optimum poundage per shovel yielding the largest day's work was established. Based upon this experiment, standardized shovels for handling different types of coal were introduced and the shovelers were instructed in how to use them. Individual output records were kept and workers who shoveled their quotas were paid significantly higher wages. Those who failed to produce up to standard were given further instruction. Those who continued to underproduce were considered unfit for the job.

Simultaneously, Taylor introduced changes in management tasks. Foremen were required to plan the next day's work in advance. When the workers arrived in the morning, they received a slip of paper detailing their predetermined tasks. Then they were sent to collect the appropriate tool and set to work promptly. In this way, no time was wasted.

Many workers, of course, resented being observed, timed, and made to work to order. Managers also objected to the additional discipline demanded. Yet Taylor and his associates could demonstrate that "Scientific Management" increased productivity. In the case of Bethlehem Steel, Taylor was able to sustain output with a much smaller labor force, cutting the cost of shoveling a ton of coal in half. Taylor insisted that workers should be rewarded for this surplus with higher wages. By linking higher wages to higher output, Taylor hoped to get labor and management to work cooperatively. While Masur admits that this may sound like "ideological bilge introduced to disguise the cruel features of the Taylor system," in fact "it was the prophecy of a new period in industrial relations."[20] Scientific Management came to be admired by capitalists and communists alike and its methods were adopted widely, especially during the First World War and in the period following the Russian Revolution, times when increasing productivity was crucial to national survival.

Time and Motion Study

Taylor's techniques were expanded upon by his contemporaries Frank Gilbreth (1868–1924), a contracting engineer, and his wife, Lillian Gilbreth (1878–1972), a psychologist. The Gilbreths' approach to work study was similar to that of Taylor, but perhaps had a more human touch. Certainly two of the Gilbreths' twelve children portray their father's fascination with efficiency in a humorous light. In their reminiscences of family life, which were dramatized in the book and films *Cheaper by the Dozen*, Frank Gilbreth Jr. and Ernestine Gilbreth Carey recall that

> at home or on the job, Dad was always the efficiency expert. He buttoned his vest from the bottom up, instead of from the top down, because the bottom-to-top process took him only three seconds, while the top-to-bottom took seven. He even used two shaving brushes to lather his face, because he found that by so doing he could cut seventeen seconds off his shaving time. For a while he tried shaving with two razors, but he finally gave that up.
>
> "I can save forty-two seconds," he grumbled, "but I wasted two minutes this morning putting this bandage on my throat." It

wasn't the slashed throat that really bothered him. It was the two minutes."[21]

While the Gilbreths were concerned with saving time, economizing on motion was even more important to them. Frank Gilbreth had started his career in construction as a bricklayer. Not surprisingly, one of the couple's most famous case studies had to do with improving the efficiency of this task. The Gilbreths were able to reduce the number of motions in ordinary bricklaying from eighteen to five, thereby increasing production from 120 to 350 bricks per hour. This was accomplished by designing a deep mortar box and an adjustable-height table on which the bricks to be laid were placed. The new table kept the bricks and mortar at the right level as the wall went up, eliminating the need to bend over. The mortar box allowed the bricklayer to scoop up a trowelful of mortar with the right hand while picking up a brick with the left. This simultaneous two-handed operation further economized on time and motion.[22]

This type of assignment led the Gilbreths to the concept of the "Therblig," a made-up term used to denote a unit of work action. The Gilbreths distilled these basic units into seventeen generic actions such as "grasp," "position," and "assemble."[23] Ordinary tasks could then be broken into sequences of Therbligs, as in the following example.

Suppose a man goes into the bathroom to shave. We'll assume that his face is all lathered and he is ready to pick up his razor. He knows where the razor is, but first he must locate it with his eye. That is "search," the first Therblig. His eye finds it and comes to rest—that's "find," the second Therblig. Third comes "select," the process of sliding the razor prior to the fourth Therblig, "grasp." Fifth is "transport loaded," bringing the razor up to the face, and sixth is "position," getting the razor set on the face. . . . .[24]

Once the Therbligs involved in a task had been identified, the Gilbreths manipulated these basic units, eliminating unnecessary actions, combining steps, and resequencing elements for greater efficiency. The aim was to find the so-called "one best way" to do the job. This optimum method was not only defined by speed but also by ease. While Taylor was mostly concerned to increase productivity, the Gilbreths were equally concerned about saving labor. Taylor preferred to study the worker with the greatest output. Gilbreth, on the other hand, would always begin by "announcing he wanted to photograph the motions of the laziest man on the job."[25] Gilbreth's premise, apparently, was that lazy workers were often the most efficient because they were too indolent to waste motion.

Gilbreth was also a pioneer in the use of cinematography in work study, being the first to analyze surgical operations by this means. He also employed stereographic still photography techniques. By "using a clock, small blinking lights attached to the subject's moving hands, a grid to calculate distance, and stereo cameras," Gilbreth was able to record a worker's movements, mapping them against time and space variables.[26] Gilbreth called these photos "chronocyclegraphs" and saw them as a kind of time-motion writing. The images are reminiscent of the geometric graphs of movement produced by Marey, in which the subject disappears. In Gilbreth's photos, too, the laboring worker becomes an indistinct blur while his or her movements are recorded as a tracery of light.

These photos can be seen as a visual metaphor of the early work study movement. Taylor and the Gilbreths devoted their efforts to the enlightened rationalization of labor. By applying the scientific method, these pioneers aimed to enhance industrial efficiency and productivity and, by so doing, to create "an earthly paradise based upon technical ingenuity."[27] In this utopian vision, the greatest happiness of the greatest number was to be obtained by producing the greatest number of goods as quickly and easily as possible. Maximum industrial production depended upon the mechanization and standardization of labor, and the human worker was simply another factor to be engineered. While Taylor and the Gilbreths were not rapacious exploiters of labor, they tended to regard the worker as a nondescript productive presence upon which standardized patterns of efficient actions were to be inscribed. As the individual features of work were systematically obliterated in the name of science, critics began to complain that something vital was being overlooked.

Intangible Aspects of Work

What was being lost was the intangible something that gives work value. As Masur avows, the time and motion specialists were not oblivious to the loss of significance that was likely to accompany the standardization and depersonalization of work. They simply believed this loss would be "compensated for by higher wages and long hours of leisure."[28] Other observers, however, noticed that the dreary side of mechanical labor tended to drain the vitality from leisure activities as well. As one eastern European noted, "I saw

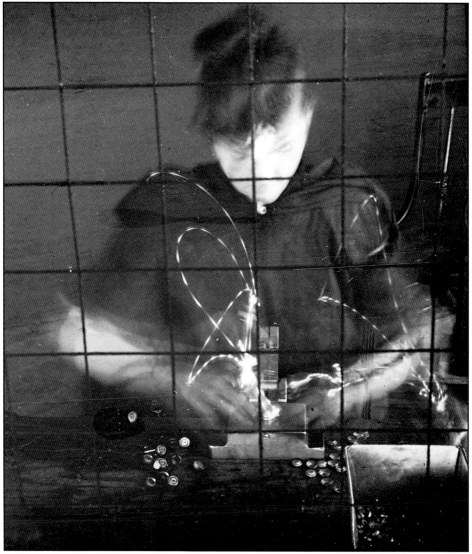

Frank Gilbreth searched for the "one best way to do the job" by using photographic techniques to trace the movement of a worker's hands through time and space.

movement and liveliness deteriorate in my homeland, where the dark paws of the machine age dragon advanced step by step in crushing the gaiety and colorful solemnity of the people."[29]

Physiologists were also among those who took issue with the engineers' tendency to view workers as adaptable machines. For example, the French physiologist and psychologist Jean-Marie Lahy criticized Taylor's ignorance of basic human physiology. Lahy pointed out that labor in modern factories involved mental as well as physical effort. Scientific Management failed to address the fatiguing effects of monotonous labor on mind and body. Consequently, Taylor's emphasis on maximum productivity and work quotas "jeopardized the health and safety of workers."[30] Trade unions in particular were sensitive to the possibility that Scientific Management would lead to the ruthless speeding up of production and often resisted the introduction of scientific work study practices, seeing them as a concealed form of surveillance, control, and exploitation.

These negative uses were not what Taylor or the Gilbreths intended. Rather, they expected improvements in the material conditions of labor to result in greater productivity and consequent improvements in the standard of living and health of the workers. Yet subsequent research by industrial engineers revealed that material conditions were not the only factors affecting output. For example, in 1927 industrial engineers set up a study of the effects of illumination on productivity at the Western Electric Company plant in Hawthorne, Illinois. Two groups were created and the illumination was varied for one group but not for the other. Surprisingly, the output of both groups increased. A second series of experiments varied wages, rest periods, temperature, and other factors. Productivity continued to increase no matter how the physical conditions were varied. Social scientist Elton Mayo concluded that merely being the subject of an experiment altered attitudes of workers and conveyed a sense of being important. The positive results of this change in attitude, known as the Hawthorne Effect, indicated that psychological variables affected productivity as much as physical ones.[31]

As the science of work study matured, it became clear that there were "imponderabilia in human life which escape the engineering mind."[32] The pioneers of photography and time and motion study had succeeded in applying an analytical method to the study of human movement and physical labor. This resulted in standardized work procedures that increased productivity. But the engineers had failed to address mental labor, to account for fatigue and monotony, or to consider psychological and social aspects of work. These were the challenges facing the next generation. And it was the unlikely partnership of a British accountant and a Hungarian dancer that would take the next steps forward.

Endnotes

1. James R. Farr, *World Eras: Industrial Revolutions in Europe 1750–1914* (Detroit: Thomson Gale, 2003), 131.

2. For more on the contrast between preindustrial and industrial conditions, see Farr, *World Eras*, 131–152.

3. Peter N. Stearns and John H. Hinshaw, *The ABC-CLIO World History Companion to the Industrial Revolution* (Santa Barbara, CA: ABC-CLIO, 1996).

4. See Farr, *World Eras*.

5. For more on this discussion, see Jean-Luc Daval, *Photography: History of an Art* (New York: Rizzoli, 1982), 61–81.

6. Ibid., 68.

7. Michel Frizot, "Movement and Duration," 243–257, in *A New History of Photography*, ed. Michel Frizot (Cologne, Germany: Konemann, 1998), 248.

8. Ibid.

9. Anson Rabinbach, *The Human Motor* (Berkeley, CA: University of California Press, 1992), 103.

10. Beaumont Newhall, *The History of Photography* (New York: New York Graphic Society Books, 1982), 121.

11. Frizot, "Movement and Duration," 250.

12. Ibid.

13. Daval, *Photography*, 74.

14. Rabinbach, *The Human Motor*, 116.

15. Ibid., 239.

16. Gerhard Masur, *Prophets of Yesterday* (New York: Macmillan, 1961), 383.

17. Frederick Winslow Taylor, quoted in Masur, *Prophets of Yesterday,* 382.

18. Frederick Winslow Taylor, "Scientific Management," 124–146, in *Organizational Theory*, ed. D. S. Pugh (Harmondsworth, England: Penguin Books, 1971), 132.

19. Taylor, "Scientific Management," 132–133.

20. Masur, *Prophets of Yesterday*, 386–387.

21. Frank B. Gilbreth Jr. and Ernestine Gilbreth Carey, *Cheaper by the Dozen* (New York: Wheeler Books, 1948), 3.

22. This case study was recounted by Taylor in his testimony before the U.S. Congress in 1912.

23. Milton L. Blum, *Industrial Psychology and Its Social Foundation* (New York: Harper and Brothers, 1949), 208.

24. Gilbreth and Carey, *Cheaper by the Dozen*, 135.

25. Ibid., 134.

26. Vicki Goldberg and Robert Silberman, *American Photography: A Century of Images* (San Francisco: Chronicle Books, 1999), 51.

27. Masur, *Prophets of Yesterday*, 388.

28. Ibid., 390.

29. Rudolf Laban, "What Has Led You to Study Movement?" *Laban Art of Movement Guild News Sheet*, No. 7 (September 1951), 7–8.

30. Rabinbach, *The Human Motor*, 250.

31. For more on the Hawthorne Effect, see J. A. C. Brown, "The Social Psychology of Industry," 302–305, in *Management and Motivation*, eds., Victor Vroom and Edward Deci (Harmondsworth, England: Penguin Books, 1970).

32. Masur, *Prophets of Yesterday*, 391.

2 INDUSTRIAL RHYTHM

August 1941

Europe was at war. As the Germans advanced across the continent, Britain was engaged in a desperate and lonely struggle for survival, pouring every ounce of its industrial strength into the war effort. One of the first management consultants in England, Frederick C. Lawrence (1895–1982), was part of this battle on the home front. With many men away in the fighting forces, women were taking on male jobs in heavy industry. As a time and motion specialist, it was Lawrence's job to advise on this transition. The critical importance of the assignment led Lawrence to take a highly unusual step— he invited a dancer into his clients' factories to give advice on efficiency.

The dancer in question was also highly unusual. His name was Rudolf Laban (1879–1958). Hungarian by birth, Laban had arrived in England in 1938, a part of the artistic diaspora provoked by the rise of fascism on the continent. Laban had been a prominent figure in the avant garde dance scene in Germany, staging modern choreographies for the theatre, running dance schools, developing lay dance practices for large groups of amateurs, and creating a notation system that allowed dances of different genres to be recorded in symbols. Upon his arrival in England, Laban had been taken under the wing of the Elmhirst family, who owned an estate in Devon known as Dartington Hall. Frederick Lawrence also had contacts at Dartington, having advised on the efficiency of estate enterprises in the late 1930s. According to historian F. M. G. Willson, it was Christopher Martin, the Dartington arts administrator, who introduced the two men, suggesting that Laban might be able to help Lawrence. In August 1941, Lawrence wrote to Laban:

> In the study of movement in industrial operations we have found the utmost difficulty in making useful records, either by description or by sketches, and it seems to me that the notation you have invented for the ballet might be applied to my work with very considerable benefit.[1]

Lawrence followed up this intitial contact by sending C. J. Cole, his chief assistant, to meet Laban. On the basis of that meeting, a one-week course in notation for Lawrence's niece, Joan Lawrence, was set up. Encouraged by the outcome of these encounters, Lawrence and Laban embarked on a collaborative factory study late in the autumn of 1941. By January 1942, the two men had a business agreement, and a new approach to the analysis of work movement was being born.[2]

The unlikely partnership of Rudolf Laban (left) and F. C. Lawrence (right) proved to be synergistic, with each man's talent and background complementing the other's.

It was an unlikely partnership. Laban was a charismatic bohemian. Aside from early studies in visual art, he was a self-made man with no professional qualifications. His lifestyle was unconventional and his knowledge of industrial practices derived almost entirely from what he had picked up while directing a festival of craft and industry in Vienna in 1929. Lawrence, on the other hand, was self-effacing and practical. He held professional qualifications as an accountant and an engineer. His Manchester-based consulting firm had been providing advice on costing and factory organization since 1923. Lawrence's command of conventional practices in time and motion study was thoroughly professional and up to date.

On the other hand, Laban's understanding of human movement was equally comprehensive and profound. Having traveled widely from boyhood, Laban possessed keen powers of observation. He had applied these not only to dance but also to what has come to be called "body language." Consequently, there was an elegant theoretical framework underlying his notation system, one that encompassed the elements of body usage, spatial design, and movement dynamics in thorough and precise detail. In addition to his gifts as a dance notator and movement analyst, Laban was something of a philosopher and reformer. He was not content for dance to be merely an entertaining display of aesthetic athleticism. Rather he meant to uncover the deeper meaning in movement and to restore the dignity of dance as an integrative and rejuvenating human endeavor.

In his own way, Lawrence was a visionary as well. He had developed an innovative accounting procedure known as marginal costing that is still used today. He also started a management school well ahead of anyone else in Britain. Moreover, it was Lawrence's dissatisfaction with conventional time and motion practices that led him to seek out Laban. While many accounts portray Laban as the guiding genius and Lawrence as the admiring sidekick who was "so attached to Laban as to hang on his every word,"[3] the two men's strengths were complementary and their working partnership of mutual benefit. Through close collaboration, these two very different characters created an approach to work analysis that incorporated mental as well as physical labor, addressed issues of fatigue, and attempted to restore personal and social meaning to factory work. The heart of this new approach was the concept of industrial rhythm.

Industrial Rhythm and Human Effort

Prior to his collaboration with Laban, Lawrence appears to have been using methods of work study similar to those employed by the Gilbreths. Industrial functions were broken into component parts in order to find ways to enhance speed and economize on motion. However, Lawrence had become skeptical about the approach. He was critical of how the "one best way" to do the job was assessed in terms of objectivity and method. He had come to feel that there was an overemphasis on time and speed and a lack of appreciation for other aspects of movement.[4]

Laban corroborated Lawrence's impressions in several important ways. Methodologically, Laban's notation system allowed for a more precise recording of details of work actions than did the Gilbreths' system of

"Therbligs." Notating work in Therbligs reduced the stream of motion to a stereotypic sequence of generic acts. Labanotation preserved individual details. Lawrence relates an interesting anecdote that illustrates this difference. In an early study, Laban was unable to visit the factory and sent a student to notate in his place. Soon afterward Lawrence and Laban reported on their findings. The audience knew that Laban had not seen the workers personally. Thus they "were amazed to see Laban himself perform every movement of each individual worker—two or three dozen of them—and to hear him prescribe improved ways of organizing their work."[5] It was a striking demonstration of the power of notation.

Secondly, the conventional time and motion study emphasized elimination of motions as a key to efficiency. The approach was quite reductionistic. Yet

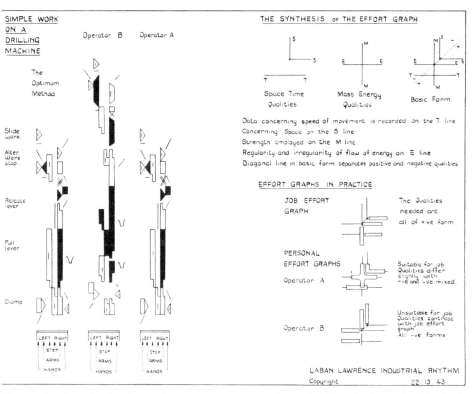

The application of Laban's notation system to the analysis of drilling is shown in this chart. Columns of symbols (left) record steps and movements of the arms and hands, contrasting the optimum method with the observed actions of two workers. On the right, the optimum effort rhythm is recorded in a graphlike notation. Effort rhythms of the two operators are recorded and assessments of each operator's suitability for the job are noted.

when Laban and Lawrence compared notations of individual workers with their output records, they did not find that the least number of motions necessarily correlated with the greatest productivity. In fact, they found that the reverse was sometimes the case. This led them to look much more closely at the nature of the movements.

On the theoretical level, Laban's concepts of "eukinetics" or "effort" proved of value. "Effort" referred to the types of kinetic energies utilized by the mover to accomplish the task. While Taylor and the Gilbreths had been preoccupied with speed, Laban considered three other elements in addition: the flow or relative degree of control needed, the variations in pressure that were required, and the straight or flexible pathways demanded by the manipulation of materials and focused use of tools. Laban's analytical framework was more refined than those previously employed. Work was not seen as being simply slow or fast, but as consisting of a variety of effort rhythms. It was the patterning of these industrial rhythms that provided the key to improving efficiency, reducing fatigue, and increasing job satisfaction.

The importance of this concept of rhythm should not be underestimated. Therefore, it is worth quoting extensively from the following unpublished manuscript in which Laban and Lawrence observe that working actions are not as simple as they may seem.

> Take the lifting of an object of a certain weight. Everybody will at once realize that to do this job, a certain strength is needed. It would seem to be a simple thing to select a person for this job who has the necessary muscular strength. Trials could also be made and if the operator is able to lift the amount of weight in question, one might think that the job can be entrusted to him. In reality, however, the case will not be so simple. The repeated lifting of a heavy weight demands not only strength, but also endurance, and, what is more important, a certain rhythmical regularity which enables the perfomer to do a series of liftings with a wise alternation of exertion and relaxation. The exact timing of the subsequent lifting exertions is one of the most important prerequisites of endurance. But not only strength and capacity of right timing comes into question. In the lifting or transporting of an object, distances, space-directions and the right way to use various paths in space are of the same importance as time and strength.

The whole effort is thus a compound of the right strength, directness, and quickness.

In the assembling of a delicate machine, where no strength at all, but a fine touch is mainly needed, the precision with which the parts of the machine must be put together requires an exact space effort and a sustained guidance of the movements of the hands which might alternate with quick grips and handlings.[6]

The authors point out that despite obvious differences in these two activities, rhythm is a common feature. Rhythm itself is composed of varying combinations of strength, time, and space. Thus these effort elements can be thought of as the common denominator of all work actions.

Laban and Lawrence underscore the implications of this discovery:

The common factor of the rhythm contained in all efforts enables us to look at them from a central point of view. It is obvious that the practical use of effort assessment in the various forms of industrial production, control, and planning must be preceded by an exact investigation of the effort rhythm in various jobs.[7]

Rhythm and Efficiency

The theory and methodology of investigating effort rhythm was initially tested at the Tyresoles factory in Manchester, where rubber tires were repaired and recycled for further use. This was a venture of importance to the war effort, due to the difficulty of getting rubber. Moreover, the factory had been forced to replace a number of men with women, who were struggling to do their jobs, especially those involving heavy lifting.

Laban's initial report on conditions in the factory was not encouraging. Laban observed undue strain and fatigue and improper handling of the tires, leading to "habits of movement which are apt to endanger health."[8] His antidote was to propose an experimental program of movement retraining. Six women were selected for the training. Over the course of one week, these women participated in two 45-minute movement sessions daily. Exercises had been designed to emphasize the qualities of movement demanded by each of the tire recycling operations. For example, lifting and carrying the tires demanded strength, a firm stance, appropriate positioning of the center of gravity, and endurance. Buffing, on the other hand, required sensitiveness of touch and thoroughness. Initial movement sessions, which were conducted away from the factory floor, focused on stability through the lower body; mobility of arms, shoulders, and spine; hand exercises for sensitiveness, grip, and release; variation in relaxation and tension; and proper respiration. These were followed by exercises performed with tires of varying weights. Later sessions were actually conducted in the factory. According to the Paton Lawrence & Co. report, the movement classes were well received by the women, who reported feeling invigorated and refreshed after the exercise sessions. "Work goes much more quickly then," one commented; while another noted that, "It is amazing how it helps you if you understand what you do."[9]

This more general movement training was then transferred to specific factory functions, such as hanging heavy tires on pegs. This had been a job that required two women straining and pushing to maneuver the tire to the height of the peg. Laban instructed the operators to swing the tire instead, so that it was carried by its own momentum to the desired height. The operator also had to support the tire at the right instant. This required little strength but involved "the faculty of suddenly changing the sustained free-flowing effort used during the swinging into a bound flow in order to stop the motion."[10] By this alteration in effort rhythm, Laban and Lawrence discovered that only one woman was required where two had previously struggled with the task.

Similar methods were employed at the Tyresoles factory in Wembly, apparently with good effect. The *Wembly Weekly* reported the influence of industrial rhythm in the following manner:

> To coin the phrase "The Greeks had a name for it" is the nearest approach to describing the "goings on" in the Works as a result of the Rhythmic Exercises. These exercises are being keenly followed. It seems that Atalanta can learn a thing or two about speed and rhythm right now. (Ed: Erring husbands will note with alarm the practised way in which our "sylphs" can swing heavy objects.)[11]

In addition to retraining women for jobs formerly handled by men, Laban and Lawrence applied the study of effort rhythm to incentive schemes. In an assignment stretching from 1942 to 1946, Laban and Lawrence worked for W. C. Holmes & Company. This foundry had been utilizing a piecework and bonus system that had caused unrest among the workers. To redress these problems, Laban and Lawrence applied a kind of trait and factor theory. The effort factors needed for each assembly line function were established. Then effort assessments of individual workers were made. The aim was to find a good match between the job factors and traits of the workers, so that each laborer could be given the job for which "he was most compatible in terms of effort."[12] Remuneration was still linked to production, but effort assessment was allied with the payment scheme. Supervision was enhanced through the understanding of effort, and management of the men improved as a consequence.[13]

Rhythm and the Prevention of Fatigue

In 1942, Laban and Lawrence were also called in to advise on agricultural production at the Dartington Estates. Land Army girls—city girls who were sent to work on farms to replace men who had enlisted—were engaged there to pick cherries, which were layered in baskets. But customers had complained that the cherries were of uneven ripeness. Those on the lower level of the basket were ripe, while upper levels were not. The foremen felt the girls simply were careless. But observations of the picking operation suggested another cause. As the girls began to pick, their movements were "determined and relatively regular."[14] But after picking for a while, their movements "became erratic and undecided" and the girls began to run uncertainly from tree to tree.[15] Laban suspected that fatigue was the cause of this obvious change in effort quality, and indeed, eyestrain was found to be the culprit. As the girls' eyes grew tired, they became unable to discern red and ripe cherries from unripe yellow ones. Once the girls were instructed to shut or relax their eyes periodically, not only were they able to fill the baskets with ripe cherries, they were able to fill the baskets more quickly.

Similar fatigue-related problems were discerned by Laban in an assignment for the Mars Company in 1943. Paton Lawrence had been called in because of high turnover, absenteeism, and morale problems among the women who wrapped the Mars bars. This hand-wrapping operation had been systematized by time and motion experts, who had as usual been concerned with minimizing movement to maximize speed. As a result, "neck, shoulder, and backache were common."[16] To make matters worse, the women were paid on a piecework basis: the more bars wrapped, the higher their pay. As a consequence, they were loathe to take a break or stretch or in any way interrupt work on the unrelenting conveyor belt.

In the cramped quality of this exacting function, Laban observed an overuse of the upper body and a concentrated posture that impeded proper breathing. Periods of relaxation alone would not redress these problems. Instead, some form of recuperation needed to be built into the wrapping operation itself. Laban felt that greater involvement of the whole body was called for to sustain the delicate and precise finger and hand movements. He found a way to integrate weight shifts from foot to foot into the initial reach for the candy bar on the conveyor belt. To counteract the cramped precision of wrapping, Laban developed "a flexible movement involving the upper part of the body."[17] Through carefully considered changes in effort rhythm and body usage, strain was reduced without diminishing productivity.

Laban's premise was that rhythmic variety and dynamic contrast were recuperative. "If the job required a downward pressure," according to biographer Valerie Preston-Dunlop, then Laban "introduced, somewhere in the movement phrase, an upward movement and released pressure. If a twist to the left were necessary, one to the right should be added."[18] This was a contrast to the standard approach in which efficiency experts eliminated actions, for Laban had realized that some of the seemingly unnecessary movements served a recuperative function. He did not see relaxation as the absence of effort. Rather, Laban believed that relaxation "involved effort."[19] And if relaxation was to be recuperative, it required the right sort of effort, one that contrasted the kind of kinetic energies primarily used in the main working exertion. While operations might take longer when recuperative actions were added, "the operator would be able to sustain work throughout the shift so that at the end of the day output was increased and the worker would feel less like a robot and more like a whole person."[20] This at least was the line of argument that Laban and Lawrence put forward. Rhythm not only enhanced productivity and diminished fatigue, it also made the very act of working more pleasurable and more meaningful. Thus, by restoring a healthy rhythm of exertion and recuperation, the two men hoped to redress the deadening effects of mechanical labor.

Rhythm and Job Satisfaction

As noted in the previous chapter, the initial attempts to engineer human factors in industry had succeeded in increasing productivity and streamlining work functions. But, as Masur opines, "Taylor and his followers were prone to close their eyes to the dreary side of industrialization and technocracy."[21] All too often, in his view, working men and women were converted into mere moving parts in a machinery they did not understand and could not control.

While the engineers could produce material plenty, they could not fill the moral and aesthetic emptiness that accompanied mechanical labor. As Masur goes on to comment, "Meaningless work is not conducive to meaningful leisure. It voids the human personality . . . it cripples the human mind."[22]

Laban and Lawrence seem to have held similar views. During his boyhood in Eastern Europe, Laban had witnessed the impact of rapid industrialization. As he recalled,

> When I was a child, peasant dances, religious processions, court ceremonials and similar movement manifestations were still alive in my home country. They were not only alive, but an integral part of social existence. If one grows up surrounded by people to whom forceful and gay, solemn and deeply felt, leisure-time activity is an important part of life, one cannot fail to be impressed by the richness of such events . . . Work itself was in those happy times and places accompanied by plenty of singing and gaiety. Everybody was proud to carry the body well during work and to do the skilled working movements in a definite rhythm. There was a great variety of bodily movement in work, and one was glad to have the opportunity to perform it in a sensible and meaningful manner.
>
> But there was also a certain anxiety in my early experiences, because I felt the relatively quick decay through the impact of modern civilization. . . . I had the opportunity to observe the workmen toiling on the new bridge. Huge cylinders of iron were sunk into the very deep river and there was no more song on the lips of the labourers who descended into these dreadful tubes. Some of them were pulled out, half-fainting, with greenish faces, and there was no energy left for gay dancing.[23]

Lawrence was equally concerned with the negative consequences of mass production. In a memo to his employees dated March 29, 1943, he decries the "ugly, gaudy, and nondescript" quality of mass-produced British goods and the consequent public disinterest in the arts. He notes that factories are not calculated to stimulate a desire for good design, as little or no attempt is made to cultivate in the working person "an appreciation of the design and working abilities of his own body and mind."[24] If workers were made aware of their movement potential, "not only would their work improve, but they would seek also to enjoy better their leisure and would become much more amenable to appreciation of design and art."[25]

For Laban and Lawrence, rhythm was the key to recovering the dignity and satisfaction inherent in a job well done. Laban was quoted as saying, *"Community rhythm makes men happy. Community rhythm is lost in industry, and we must either find it again or replace it by something equally satisfying."*[26] Whenever Laban and Lawrence ran movement training programs with workers, they usually recommended that employers establish recreational movement classes as well, "to give compensation for the physical strain at work."[27] There is, however, little indication that client companies implemented this recommendation. Laban and Lawrence had to content themselves with whatever could be done to make the job itself more satisfying.

One way to make work more satisfying was to place workers in jobs for which they showed some innate movement aptitude. The assumption was that it is more rewarding to perform actions that come naturally than to be constrained to make efforts that lie outside the normal movement repertoire. Laban had found that when workers were so constrained, they often performed poorly and showed signs of stress. For example, a worker whose natural rhythm was slow and contemplative was likely to become irritable in a conveyor belt operation demanding fast and automatic action. Such a worker was better suited to handwork, such as finishing, in which "his latent craftsmanship" would find "natural expression" in slower movement and more thoughtful action.[28] Consequently, when Laban and Lawrence went into a company, individual assessments of workers were made and then the workers were sorted into three groups: those who were in a job for which they were well suited, those who could learn to do the job through movement retraining, and those for whom some other job should be found. On the basis of these assessments, workers would be retrained and reassigned.

This type of assessment and reassignment was done on a large scale in the bottling department of the Glaxo pharmaceutical company in 1951. The innate effort rhythms of close to 300 women were assessed. Based on these analyses, most workers were moved to different jobs. When the dust settled, "productivity increased over 30%" and this improvement was maintained, suggesting that the workers found the new assignments more to their liking.[29]

Another approach to enhancing job satisfaction involved introducing teamwork in production. Since the invention of the moving assembly line, it had been a standard industrial practice to break the manufacturing process into discrete and simple operations that could be done by semi-skilled workers.

This was the situation Laban and Lawrence found in the Faithful Overalls Company in the early 1950s. One seamstress produced pockets all day, another only sewed on snaps, and so on. Such repetitive piecework was tediously dull. So in addition to assessing and reassigning the 200 Faithful Overalls workers, Laban and Lawrence created teams of ten. Each team produced a whole garment and each member of the team was taught to do at least two operations. Wage benefits were attached to improved performance, and the more productive teams were rewarded. Productivity increased. Moreover, according to Davies, "Workers, almost without exception, said how much they liked being in a team."[30]

Fifty years on, it is difficult to corroborate claims linking selection by means of effort and teamwork to job satisfaction. Nevertheless, it is clear that both Laban and Lawrence were concerned with the more intangible aspects of the work experience. Some of their interventions prefigure more contemporary approaches, such as "Employee Wellness Programs" and "Quality Circles" that also attempt to enhance the psychological and social aspects of the workplace.

Mental Effort

The initial assignments handled by Laban and Lawrence focused on manual labor in manufacturing and agriculture. By gradual increments, other types of jobs began to be studied. Archival traces show that by the summer of 1943 Laban and Lawrence were contemplating extending their rhythmic studies to clerical and managerial posts. In an unpublished manuscript, the two men noted that the visibility of rhythmic movement was diminished in white collar labor, for "the nervous system is more strained than the muscular system." Nevertheless, they observed that clerks and managers "use a working rhythm and consume rhythmical energy."[31] Though the work may be more mental than physical, Laban and Lawrence emphasized that "certain tests made in connection with selection have shown that thoughts have:

Speed
Strength
Direction
Flow."[32]

This is a rather surprising assertion. Earlier work study experts had not attempted to delineate intellectual functions in movement terms. For Taylor, there was a great divide between men suited to work with their hands and those equipped to do brainier tasks. Of the seventeen generic Therbligs outlined by the Gilbreths, only three could be related remotely to mental labor: "select," "inspect," and "plan." But Laban and Lawrence were suggesting that the effort factors used to analyze manual labor could also be applied to study mental labor. They admitted that clerical and managerial movements were subtle and the rhythms less obvious than those used in more manual jobs. Nevertheless, they found "scope enough for assessment of effort."[33]

Laban and Lawrence claimed that this assertion was based on empirical study and testing. But it should really be recognized as a theoretical breakthrough in the science of work study. No longer were physical and intellectual labors discrete, nor was one more privileged than the other. Instead, effort rhythm was seen to underlie all human endeavor. The difference between physical and mental labor was not one of kind but merely one of scale. The stage was set for the study of managerial function through the analysis of movement.

By the late 1940s, Laban and Lawrence had begun applying techniques developed for the study of manual labor to the assessment of management action. Marketed first as the Personal Effort Assessment and later as the Laban-Lawrence Test, the procedure was similar to that used with factory workers. Managers were observed on the job or in a job interview, and movement notations were made. Then these observations were analyzed to produce a profile of the candidate, outlining his strengths, weaknesses, and latent capacities. This profile was compared to the job specifications. Finally, recommendations were made as to the individual's suitability for a particular post.

While the procedure used was similar to that used with factory workers, adjustments had to be made in the type and scale of movements observed and the interpretation of these actions. How correlations were drawn between movement data and managerial aptitude is not obvious in early reports, however, and the work can be assumed to have been quite experimental. The quality of advice given must have depended in part upon Laban's legendary intuition and personal charm. Nevertheless, rudiments of an observational methodology and interpretive framework for understanding management behavior were being laid out by Laban and Lawrence. And they were training the young man who was destined to extend the system from the factory floor to the executive suite. His name is Warren Lamb. The next chapter in the development of industrial rhythm belongs to him.

Endnotes

1. F. M. G. Willson, *In Just Order Move: The Progress of the Laban Centre for Movement and Dance, 1946–1996* (London: Athlone Press, 1996), 19.

2. F. C. Lawrence, Letters to Rudolf Laban, August 1941–January 1942, National Resource Centre for Dance (NRCD) Laban Archive, ref. nos. E(L)/66/22, E(L)/66/23.

3. Eden Davies, *Beyond Dance: Laban's Legacy of Movement Analysis* (London: Brechin Books, 2001), 37.

4. Rudolf Laban and F. C. Lawrence, "Effort," NRCD Laban Archive, ref. no. E(L)/53/1, 4b.

5. F. C. Lawrence, "From Far and Near," *Laban Art of Movement Guild Magazine* (December 1954), 26–27.

6. Rudolf Laban and F. C. Lawrence, "Short Description of Rhythmic Effort Assessment," March 9, 1942, NRCD Laban Archive, ref. no. E(L)/65/66.

7. Ibid.

8. Rudolf Laban, "Report upon the Experimental Work Carried out at Tyresoles Limited," NRCD Laban Archive, ref. no. E(L)/71/2.

9. Ibid.

10. Rudolf Laban and F. C. Lawrence, *Effort* (London: MacDonald & Evans, 1947), 80.

11. *Wembly Weekly*, No. 21, April 22, 1942, NRCD Laban Archive, ref. no. E(L)/71/1.

12. Valerie Preston-Dunlop, *Rudolf Laban: An Extraordinary Life*

(London: Dance Books, 1998), 222.

13. Paton Lawrence & Company, "Laban Lawrence Consultations," NRCD Laban Archive, ref. no. E(L)/74/17.

14. Laban and Lawrence, *Effort*, 78.

15. Ibid.

16. Davies, *Beyond Dance*, 43.

17. Ibid, 44.

18. Preston-Dunlop, *Rudolf Laban*, 223.

19. Laban and Lawrence, *Effort*, 12.

20. Preston-Dunlop, *Rudolf Laban*, 224.

21. Gerhard Masur, *Prophets of Yesterday* (New York: Macmillan, 1961), 391.

22. Ibid.

23. Rudolf Laban, "What Has Led You to Study Movement?" *Laban Art of Movement Guild News Sheet*, No. 7 (September 1951), 7–8.

24. F. C. Lawrence, Memo to Staff, March 29, 1943, NRCD Laban Archive, ref. no. E(L)/65/32.

25. Ibid.

26. Rudolf Laban, quoted in Olive Moore, "Man of the Month," *Scope Magazine for Industry* (October 1954), 72.

27. Laban, "Report upon the Experimental Work."

28. Moore, "Man of the Month."

29. Davies, *Beyond Dance*, 74.

30. Ibid., 75.

31. Rudolf Laban and F. C. Lawrence, "The Rhythm of the Office Worker," July 31, 1943, NRCD Laban Archive, ref. no. E(L)/66/13.

32. Rudolf Laban and F. C. Lawrence, "The Rhythm of the Manager," July 19, 1943, NRCD Laban Archive, ref. no. E(L)/65/43.

33. Laban and Lawrence, "Rhythm of Office Worker."

3 FROM THE FACTORY FLOOR TO THE EXECUTIVE SUITE

The Journey Begins

Between 1941 and 1946, Laban and Lawrence pioneered the study of industrial rhythm in a variety of factory operations, ranging from hand-wrapping of Mars candy bars to the operation of cranes and loading gangs on the Manchester Ship Canal.[1] In 1947, one of Laban's movement students, Warren Lamb, became involved in this work. Lamb (1923–) had become fascinated with the study of movement after his release from the British navy, giving up a banking career to pursue studies with Laban. Laban was in the habit of passing on work to students when he was unavailable himself. And so Lamb, who had gone to Manchester to study dance, soon found himself on factory assignments:

> The usual practice was for me to work alone, standing all day in some hot steamy weaving shed, the clatter of looms making speech impossible, intensely observing and before long, trying desperately to keep my eyes open. Laban demanded lots of sheets of paper covered with effort "graphs" and I strove desperately to make copious observations of some sort or other. The usual practice was for me to take these sheets of paper to Laban, who would go through them avidly asking me penetrating questions.[2]

As Lamb recounts, these observations would be analyzed in various ways and preliminary conclusions would be reached as to which workers were suitable and which were not. Then Laban would accompany Lamb to the workplace to confirm or refute his conclusions. Through this close association with Laban, Lamb became adept at effort assessment. In 1950, he joined Paton Lawrence & Co. Lamb was involved in the job reassignment project at Glaxo and played a key role in the setting up of production teams at the Faithful Overalls factory. Gradually, other sorts of assignments came his way.

As Lamb recalls,

> The work with operatives led to the odd foreman and manager

being included. Laban had a gurulike charisma and so managers who felt themselves in some difficulty would consult him. When inconvenient to him I would find myself observing a manager's movement and sometimes writing a report. Laban used his genius for giving some point of advice which, when the manager tried it out, helped him to feel better. I used to have to try and give more chapter and verse.[3]

In a relaxed mood, Laban (left) and Lawrence (right) celebrate the ending of the war.

The categories of movement to be analyzed had been outlined by Laban and rudimentary links to the assessment of management action had been explored. But initially the interpretive process was flexible. Laban was endlessly "fashioning some new interpretation, trying out some new arrangement of data."[4] Lamb confesses that he was often mystified by Laban's approach. "It seemed to me that he came to conclusions in minutes because of his genius, while I sweated for hours trying to avoid any conclusion until a disciplined analysis and evaluation had been made."[5]

Yet it was Lamb's objective and disciplined analysis that proved crucial to making the study of industrial rhythm applicable to the assessment of senior executives. While Movement Pattern Analysis (MPA), as it is known today, stands upon the groundwork laid by Laban and Lawrence, its methodological and theoretical structures were constructed by Lamb painstakingly. Through his independent work with hundreds of individuals, Lamb clarified the parameters of movement that were relevant for assessing decision making and translated this movement information into terms that could be grasped by managers and related to their practical experience. In this way, movement study that began on the factory floor was extended to reach the executive suite. Laban and Lawrence had laid the foundation, but it took Lamb's efforts to build a grounded theory sophisticated enough to reach the top levels of management. This chapter recounts that development.

Developing a Grounded Theory

In 1953 Lamb left Paton Lawrence & Co. to set up his own consulting firm. This independence from Laban and Lawrence increased Lamb's determination to establish a better basis for the assessment work he was doing. Over the next decade he applied his considerable powers of observation to the study of management behaviors in what can best be characterized as a "grounded theory" approach.[6] Grounded theory inverts the process typically used in research. It does not start from a hypothesis and proceed to controlled experimentation. Instead, grounded theory starts from naturalistic observations taken in the field. On the basis of these observations, preliminary explanations are formulated. Then new observations are collected and the hypotheses are revised accordingly. This was the approach that Laban had been using in his initial studies of industrial rhythm, albeit informally. Observations were taken in the factories and offices, then various explanatory schemes were tried out. This was followed by more observations in the field that either confirmed or refuted initial conclusions. Lamb carried this "grounded" process on, continuing to clarify movement observation procedures while refining the interpretation of movement.

Clarifying Movement Observation Procedures. Laban had identified three categories of movement as being relevant to the assessment of managers: functional actions, shadow movements, and body attitude. Lamb, however, encountered increasing difficulty in making distinctions along these categorical lines. By gradual increments, he redefined these categories. For example, Lamb reasoned that a body attitude is a movement of the whole body; that is, a *posture*. A shadow movement, which had been defined by Laban as a small, fleeting action confined to one part of the body, could be thought of as a *gesture*.

Differentiating actions of the whole body (postures) from movements involving only one part of the body (gestures) was much simpler, Lamb found, than the earlier categorical schema. Moreover, it led to an unexpected discovery.

C. D. Ellis (left) interviews a candidate (center) for a managerial post while Warren Lamb (right) observes and notates the candidate's movement behaviors.

For assessment purposes, Lamb was looking for the "essence of a person" and trying to establish a disciplined basis for grasping this in movement terms. At the time, he was doing a lot of work with short-listed candidates for management posts, and he was very aware of the danger of being impressed just because a candidate gave a good interview. For that reason, he always had someone else do the interview. This procedure allowed him to observe and notate the candidate's movements more objectively. In this process, he noticed that people could assume postures and gestures. That is, these aspects of movement seemed to be open to conscious control and could be "managed" to create a good impression. If these movement parameters did not reflect the intrinsic characteristics of the person, Lamb reasoned, then there must be something else that was true to the person, something that could not be faked. As he observed more closely, he found this in unselfconscious moments of postural adjustment, when a fleeting congruence of posture and gesture occurred. Lamb dubbed these "posture-gesture mergers" and made these integrated movements the focus of his analysis.[8]

Refining the Interpretation of Movement. Lamb had clarified the categories

39

of bodily action to be considered for assessment purposes, but there was still the problem of interpretation. Again, Lamb was able to draw upon what he had learned from Laban, and develop it further. He recalled that in his teaching of effort Laban had

> postulated an action sequence of Attention, Intention, Decision, and Precision. Laban correlated these stages respectively with these movement elements: Attention with Space Effort (variations in focus), Intention with Weight Effort (variations in force), Decision with Time Effort (variations in speed), and Precision with Flow Effort (variations in muscular tension).[9]

While the order of the sequence was often changed around, Laban usually placed Precision, or Flow, in the final spot. This sequencing had never made sense to Lamb. It seemed more logical for Flow to start the sequence or to come in and out in a fluid manner as the action progressed.

Moreover, Lamb had felt for some time that Flow did not have equal footing with the other effort elements. This conviction grew through his work with Dr. Judith Kestenberg. Kestenberg was a child psychiatrist of the Freudian persuasion who had come to Lamb initially for movement tutoring. Subsequently Lamb became involved in her longitudinal studies of infant and toddler development.[10] What the two discovered was that Flow predominated in the movement of very young children. Then, as the children began to gain mastery of their bodily actions, Weight, Time, and Space elements appeared, and Flow diminished. This strengthened Lamb's conviction that Flow was not the same as the other elements of movement and should be interpreted independently.

Finally, Lamb was struck more and more by the way managers shaped their bodies in space. Laban had developed elaborate theories about spatial design (known as Choreutic theory), and Lamb had become familiar with these ideas in conjunction with his own study of dance. But, rather curiously, Laban had never integrated the analysis of the shape of movement into the industrial rhythm work. In 1957, Lamb approached Laban about incorporating more analysis of shape into the assessment work. Other than looking surprised by this suggestion, Laban offered no opposition. Laban's death a year later opened the way for further independent study. Lamb began to observe shaping processes seriously and to reflect on their possible role in management behavior.[11]

Framing Management Behavior. By the early 1960s Lamb had clarified the

categories of Posture, Gesture, and Posture-Gesture Merger. He had concluded that Flow should be interpreted independently of the other effort elements.
And he had begun an investigation of shaping elements. But how were these
movement elements related to the jobs that managers do? How could they be
interpreted and made relevant for selecting and placing people in jobs?

Lamb returned to Laban's concept of Attention, Intention, and Decision.
These seemed to form a logical sequence that could be related to planning and
taking action; that is, to things that managers actually do. Thus Lamb began
to outline a decision-making framework that consisted of three stages. Laban
had already hypothesized correlations of effort elements with these stages.
Lamb sought to integrate the observation of the shape of movement into the
action sequence. By combining his observations of others with reflections on
his own movement experience, Lamb was able to detect a logical sequence:

> Horizontally oriented movement puts the performer in touch
> with what is going on around him. Vertical orientation then
> emphasizes where he stands in relation to whatever he is in
> touch with. Finally comes the Sagittal orientation, a form of
> decision to advance or to retire from the subject matter.[12]

In this way, Lamb came to see effort and shape as complementary aspects
of a decision-making process. The effort elements represented an assertive
approach to Attention, Intention, and Decision (which Lamb renamed
Commitment), while the shape elements had to do with gaining perspective
at each stage.

Lamb was close now to having established a solid basis for assessing the
traits of the manager and matching these against the requirements of the job.
In regard to the latter, Lamb developed detailed job descriptions couched in
decision-making terms. He would ask, "To what extent will the new manager
have to give Attention in order to succeed?" "To what extent must he or she
Intend?" etc. Further definition would be given by examining the relative
need for assertion and perspective. By means of this type of painstaking
analysis, Lamb's theoretical correlation of movement behavior and decision-
making style gradually coalesced. In research terms, he had reached the point
at which observations in the field no longer revealed anomalies that required
explanatory adjustments. His grounded theory was complete.[13]

By 1965 Lamb felt confident that he finally had a solid basis on which to
give advice. He found himself in demand, working with many different
management teams. His client companies were drawn from all industrial

sectors and ranged in size from small partnerships to large corporations. The theory and practices arduously worked out by Laban, Lawrence, and Lamb were finally being employed at the top level. As Lamb puts it, "It was really this matching of movement against a decision-making model that enabled the leap to be made from observing operatives and workers on the plant floor to looking at managers."[14] Individual movement rhythm could be seen as a pattern of decision-making initiatives. More important, Lamb had found a way to describe these initiatives in terms that business people could readily relate to their practical management experience.

The Framework of Management Initiative: The Motivation to Act

While the *Framework of Management Initiative* has undergone minor revision and elaboration in subsequent years, its essential character is as Lamb conceived it in 1965.[15] In this conception, management action is viewed logically as a three-stage decision-making process. The process begins when the individual becomes aware that there is a need for action, and gives Attention to the matter.

Giving Attention. Lamb delineates two approaches to giving Attention: Investigating and Exploring. Investigating is the process of ferreting out information in depth within a prescribed area of scrutiny. Exploring involves looking around more broadly to ascertain what else might be of interest or relevance. These are complementary processes. By Investigating and/or Exploring, the manager generates a field of information on which well-informed action may be based, making sure that facts are accurate and that relevant resources have not been overlooked.

Forming an Intention. This stage of decision making is the bridge between initial consideration and implementation in which one settles upon an appropriate course of action. Lamb delineates two approaches to forming an Intention: Determining and Evaluating. Determining is the process of building and maintaining conviction that a given plan of action is worth pursuing. Evaluating is the process of establishing the relative importance of a course of action, so as to have a clear perspective on the issues and a realistic sense of priorities. Again, these are complementary processes. By Determining and/or Evaluating, the manager establishes the purpose and value of what he or she intends to do and makes sure that there is sufficient resolution to proceed.

Making a Commitment. This is the climax of the decision-making process in

FRAMEWORK OF MANAGEMENT INITIATIVE
THE MOTIVATION TO ACT
THE DECISION-MAKING PROCESS IN ACTION

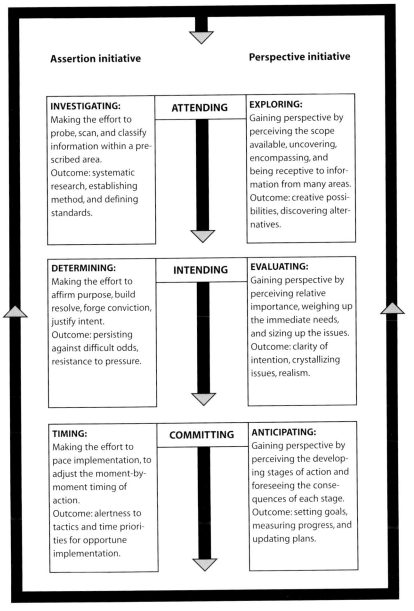

Assertion initiative   **Perspective initiative**

INVESTIGATING:
Making the effort to probe, scan, and classify information within a prescribed area.
Outcome: systematic research, establishing method, and defining standards.

ATTENDING

EXPLORING:
Gaining perspective by perceiving the scope available, uncovering, encompassing, and being receptive to information from many areas.
Outcome: creative possibilities, discovering alternatives.

DETERMINING:
Making the effort to affirm purpose, build resolve, forge conviction, justify intent.
Outcome: persisting against difficult odds, resistance to pressure.

INTENDING

EVALUATING:
Gaining perspective by perceiving relative importance, weighing up the immediate needs, and sizing up the issues.
Outcome: clarity of intention, crystallizing issues, realism.

TIMING:
Making the effort to pace implementation, to adjust the moment-by-moment timing of action.
Outcome: alertness to tactics and time priorities for opportune implementation.

COMMITTING

ANTICIPATING:
Gaining perspective by perceiving the developing stages of action and foreseeing the consequences of each stage.
Outcome: setting goals, measuring progress, and updating plans.

© Warren Lamb

43

which action is taken. Once something has been done, it cannot easily be undone. Consequently, there is always an element of risk at this stage. The two approaches to making a Commitment delineated by Lamb have to do with controlling the process of implementation through appropriate Timing and Anticipating. The process of Timing has to do with managing the pace of implementation so as to initiate action at the most opportune moment. The process of Anticipating involves strategically controlling the ongoing process of implementation to achieve long-term goals and avoid negative consequences. These are also complementary processes. By Timing and/or Anticipating, the manager chooses the right moment to act so as to achieve the desired outcome while avoiding potential pitfalls in the process of implementation. (The complete framework of action is shown on page 43.)

Profiles in Action

Every manager, and indeed every person, Investigates, Explores, Determines, Evaluates, Times, and Anticipates in the process of making decisions. Yet Lamb has found that individual managers rarely apply themselves equally to all six processes. Instead, individual managers apportion their time and energy in various ways, emphasizing some stages of decision making more than others. Thus, a pattern of preferred initiatives can be detected. This pattern, which can be represented graphically in terms of the relative magnitude of initiative taken at each stage of decision making, is a significant indicator of how the individual will handle his or her job. For example, Profile A represents an individual who emphasizes the Attention-oriented processes of Investigating and Exploring. This individual will need to feel that he or she is thoroughly informed before getting ready to act. In contrast, the individual represented by Profile B concentrates time and energy on the Commitment-oriented processes of Timing and Anticipating. This manager is likely to act first and ask questions later. Profile C, in contrast, represents a person who takes a lot of initiative to Determine and Evaluate. Such a person is only ready to act once he or she is convinced of the value and purpose of the action.

The relative emphasis on assertion or perspective will further modify the approach to decision making. For example, profiles A1 and A2 (page 46) show contrasting emphases. The individual represented in A1 gives Attention by taking a lot of initiative to Investigate, with little emphasis on Exploring. This suggests a person who will carefully delineate what is to be considered and look into that in depth, but without taking the trouble to look "outside the box." In contrast, the person represented in A2 will take a lot of initiative to Explore without making much effort to Investigate. This individual will be motivated to broaden the scope of what is being looked into, but may be imprecise about the details of the information that are being made available through these explorations. Of course, some Attention-oriented managers balance assertion and perspective, combining both depth and breadth in their approach to research.

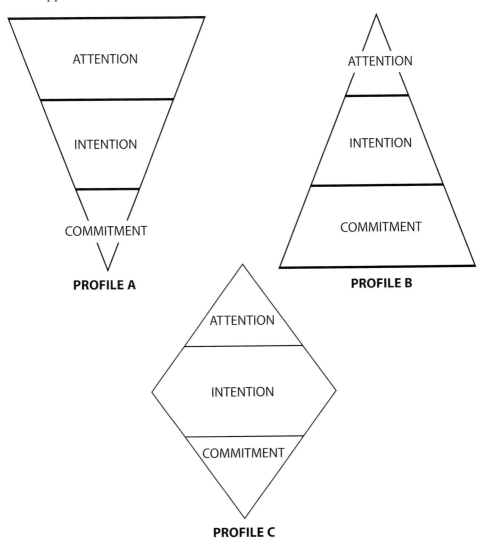

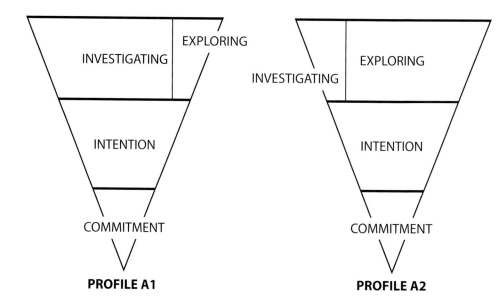

PROFILE A1   PROFILE A2

In addition to the relative emphasis on assertion and perspective in the predominant stage of decision making, the manager's approach will be modified by the concentration of time and energy in the other two stages. For example, the profile shown in B1 contrasts with that of B2. In the first instance, the manager will act first and then rationalize the action by backing it up with Intention. That is, once embarked on a course of action, this

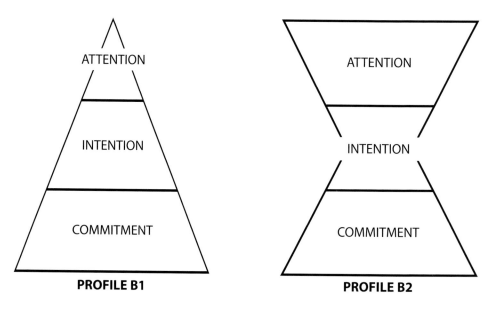

PROFILE B1   PROFILE B2

individual will not give up readily. The relatively slight emphasis on Attending suggests that action will be based more on opportunism and intuitive hunch than on solid information. The equal emphases on Attention and Commitment shown in profile B2 suggest a different approach. This individual will tend to vacillate between wanting to consider matters thoroughly and feeling compelled to jump into action. This person will take little initiative to form Intentions and may find it difficult to justify why something has been done. Faced with opposition, it will be much easier for this manager to give up than is the case with the person represented in profile B1.

Further refinements in these profiles are possible and detailed examples of Movement Pattern Analysis profiles will be discussed in the two final chapters of this book. The point to be conveyed at the moment is that patterns of movement can be correlated with a decision-making model to reflect characteristic approaches to management tasks. This pattern is a significant, though not rigidly fixed, indicator of how an individual will handle his or her job. As Lamb emphasizes,

> What is the essence of a pattern is that the pattern can move. We are not rigid beings paralyzed into a particular state. We live in a state of flux. Nevertheless, we bring a character, an individually distinct character, into that state of flux that we can understand in pattern form.[16]

No Manager Is an Island: Understanding the Initiative to Interact

The profile based upon Movement Pattern Analysis can be a viable indicator of how an individual will approach his or her job. However, the success or failure of a given manager depends upon many other contextual variables including the corporate culture, boardroom politics, and the state of the broader economic climate. Lamb has found that it is not possible to apply trait and factor theory in a simpleminded manner to the selection and placement of senior managers. It is far more sensible to look at any candidate in relation to the whole senior team. In this context, patterns of interaction are also relevant, for in complex organizations executives must not only be able to make decisions independently, they must also be able to give Attention, form Intentions, and make Commitments with and through others. As a consequence, Lamb has also applied Movement Pattern Analysis to the study of interaction style and related this interpersonal dimension of management behavior to the decision-making framework.

Lamb's initial research on interaction was elaborated in the early 1980s by colleagues who identified four fundamental interpersonal styles: sharing, private, neutral, and versatile.[17] These are described first in generic terms and then related to the decision-making framework.

Sharing Style. In this interactional approach, the individual prefers to work interdependently, making his or her initiatives available to others and also drawing on the energies of colleagues. The nature of shared initiatives varies in each stage of decision making. For example, in sharing Attention, managers Investigate and Explore together, exchanging information, generating ideas, and creating a communicative atmosphere. The effect is to make sure that everyone knows what is going on in the preliminary stage of decision making. In sharing Intention, colleagues Determine and Evaluate together. Views and opinions are kicked around, as each person presents his or her position and attempts to influence or persuade others to take a similar stand. The effect is to generate a consensus on how to move forward. In sharing Commitment, individuals Time and Anticipate together. This creates an operational atmosphere, in which the process of implementation is coordinated, with a clear vision of the goal to be attained.

Private Style. In this interactional approach, the individual prefers to work independently, keeping the decision-making process to oneself. Again, the nature of what is handled independently differs with each stage of decision making. In giving Attention privately, the manager looks into matters on his or her own, not wanting to make this information available to coworkers until the process is complete. In forming an Intention privately, the individual prefers to size up the issues and take a position without being influenced prematurely by the views of colleagues. In making a Commitment privately, the person prefers to be able to act when he or she is ready without being constrained to coordinate implementation with others.

Neutral Style. In this style, the individual is available for interaction but dependent upon the initiatives of others. Neutrality in interaction is reactive: the individual will be available to share if the other person takes the initiative, or he or she can go it alone if the other person prefers independence. When a person is neutral in Attention, he or she will take little initiative to share information but can be drawn out if another person takes the interactional lead. When an individual is neutral in Intention, he or she will

FRAMEWORK OF MANAGEMENT INITIATIVE
THE MOTIVATION TO INTERACT
THE DECISION-MAKING PROCESS IN RELATION TO OTHERS

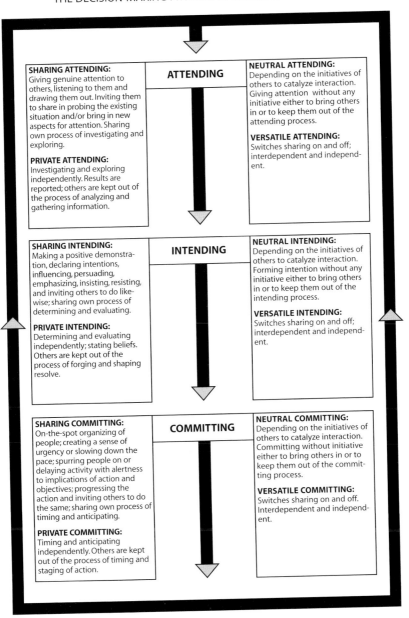

SHARING ATTENDING:
Giving genuine attention to others, listening to them and drawing them out. Inviting them to share in probing the existing situation and/or bring in new aspects for attention. Sharing own process of investigating and exploring.

PRIVATE ATTENDING:
Investigating and exploring independently. Results are reported; others are kept out of the process of analyzing and gathering information.

ATTENDING

NEUTRAL ATTENDING:
Depending on the initiatives of others to catalyze interaction. Giving attention without any initiative either to bring others in or to keep them out of the attending process.

VERSATILE ATTENDING:
Switches sharing on and off; interdependent and independent.

SHARING INTENDING:
Making a positive demonstration, declaring intentions, influencing, persuading, emphasizing, insisting, resisting, and inviting others to do likewise; sharing own process of determining and evaluating.

PRIVATE INTENDING:
Determining and evaluating independently; stating beliefs. Others are kept out of the process of forging and shaping resolve.

INTENDING

NEUTRAL INTENDING:
Depending on the initiatives of others to catalyze interaction. Forming intention without any initiative either to bring others in or to keep them out of the intending process.

VERSATILE INTENDING:
Switches sharing on and off; interdependent and independent.

SHARING COMMITTING:
On-the-spot organizing of people; creating a sense of urgency or slowing down the pace; spurring people on or delaying activity with alertness to implications of action and objectives; progressing the action and inviting others to do the same; sharing own process of timing and anticipating.

PRIVATE COMMITTING:
Timing and anticipating independently. Others are kept out of the process of timing and staging of action.

COMMITTING

NEUTRAL COMMITTING:
Depending on the initiatives of others to catalyze interaction. Committing without initiative either to bring others in or to keep them out of the committing process.

VERSATILE COMMITTING:
Switches sharing on and off. Interdependent and independent.

© Warren Lamb

49

take little initiative to persuade or influence others. If someone else initiates sharing, this person can make his or her views known. Finally, when an individual is neutral in Commitment, he or she will take little initiative to coordinate activities. But again, this person can fit into the program of action with someone else who is capable of sharing interaction at this stage.

Versatile Style. In this style, individuals combine a need to work with and through others with a need for independence. This can lead to a slightly unpredictable pattern of interaction. The versatile Attender will want to share information and draw on the ideas of others at some times and, on other occasions, will prefer to Investigate and Explore alone. Similarly, in some instances the versatile Intender will make his or her views known while at other times he or she will want to Determine a course of action and Evaluate matters without any influence from other people. Finally, the versatile Committer needs the possibility to Time and Anticipate action in concert with others, as well as the scope to handle the tactics and strategy of implementation independently. (The complete framework of interaction is shown on page 49.)

Overall Factors

Finally, Lamb identified two other factors relevant to management behavior: Dynamism and Identifying.

Dynamism has been defined as the number of novel cycles of decision making an individual will simultaneously initiate and continue. Dynamism can be thought of as the relative intensity with which an individual applies him- or herself to nonroutine decisions; that is, to matters that require real preliminary consideration, genuine grappling with issues, and adroit implementation. Less dynamically intense managers will tend to want to complete one novel decision-making process before taking another on board. There will be an inclination to handle projects *sequentially*. More dynamic managers are willing to take on more things at once. They will tend to overlap projects, having many decisions in process *simultaneously*.

Identifying has been defined as the readiness to respond, participate, and become involved in action. Identifying can be thought of as the executive's "response quotient," that is, "the level of sensitivity to the stimulus provided by the work environment."[18] Again, it is the relative magnitude of Identifying that is significant, for Identifying has been found to govern the degree of cohesiveness in a management team. When Identifying is high, reports Lamb's former partner, Pamela Ramsden, "There will be an involving, 'all in this together' atmosphere. Many things will be sparked off spontaneously, and there will be an easy, casual interchange amongst the members of the team."[19] In teams with less Identifying, a more formal atmosphere will prevail.

This explanation of Dynamism and Identifying completes the discussion of the *Framework of Management Initiative* crystallized by Lamb in the mid-1960s. It is now possible to return to the main historical line and bring the story up to the present day.

On the Cutting Edge

Crystallization of the *Framework of Management Initiative* in 1965 set the stage for its subsequent application in business and industry. At this writing, more than 30,000 individuals have been assessed.[20] Over 400 companies have utilized the approach, some for more than two decades.[21] A wide variety of books and articles have been written about Movement Pattern Analysis.[22] A score of consultants have been trained to use the method, and professional standards of qualification have been established.[23] Validation and reliability studies have been conducted.[24] Beginning with the work done by Laban and Lawrence, empirical evidence and case studies have been collected for over sixty years. During the last thirty years, Lamb's unique approach has been scrutinized by clients, other consultants, journalists, and scholars. In surveying this history, it becomes clear that the movement study work of Laban, Lawrence, and Lamb is neither "new" nor unknown.

Nevertheless, Movement Pattern Analysis is still viewed as innovative, an assessment technique situated on the cutting edge. Its perennial novelty seems to lie in its reliance on the analysis of nonverbal behavior. Even client companies who have employed the technique for decades are skeptical that management style can be understood through the medium of body movement.[25]

And yet, this is the case.

In the second part of this book, we take a closer look at the discipline of movement analysis, surveying the elements of human movement and their relationship to decision making. Case histories of the application of Movement Pattern Analysis are discussed, and the case for the efficacy of movement study is examined.

Endnotes

1. In addition to Tyresoles, the Dartington Estates agricultural operations, Mars Candy Company, and the W. C. Holmes foundry case studies reported in Chapter 2, Laban and Lawrence also did industrial rhythm assignments for Hoover, Dunlop, J. Lyons, St. Olave's Curing and Preserving, the Manchester Ship Canal, Sykes and Harrison, Barlows Ltd., and the Royal Air Force during these years. Other big assignments, like the assessment exercise with 300 operatives at Glaxo, took place in the late 1940s and early 1950s. Records in the Laban Archive held by the National Resource Centre for Dance at the University of Surrey, U.K., suggest that Laban and Lawrence surveyed a wide range of manual, clerical, and managerial functions in at least twenty-five different client companies prior to Laban's death in 1958.

2. Warren Lamb, "The Development of Action Profiling," *Action News* [Warren Lamb Associates newsletter], Winter 1980, Fall 1980, Spring 1981, Autumn 1981.

3. Lamb, "Development of Action Profiling," Winter 1980.

4. Ibid.

5. Ibid.

6. Barney Glaser and Anselm Strauss, *The Discovery of Grounded Theory* (Chicago: Aldine, 1967).

7. Warren Lamb, "The Development of Movement Pattern Analysis," lecture, Motus Humanus Advanced Seminar, Boulder, CO, August 19, 1996.

8. Warren Lamb, *Posture and Gesture* (London: Gerald Duckworth, 1965).

9. Lamb, "Development of Action Profiling," Spring 1981.

10. Judith Kestenberg, *Children and Parents: Psychoanalytic Studies in Development* (New York: Jason Aronson, 1975).

11. Lamb, "Development of Movement Pattern Analysis."

12. Lamb, "Development of Action Profiling," Spring 1981.

13. For further discussion of the completion of a grounded theory research process, see Norman Denzin, *The Research Act* (New York: McGraw-Hill, 1978); Anselm Strauss, *Qualitative Analysis for Social Scientists* (Cambridge: Cambridge University Press, 1987).

14. Lamb, "Development of Movement Pattern Analysis."

15. Various terms have been changed over the years. For example, "Evaluating" was called "Confronting" and "Timing" was known as "Deciding" prior to 1982. The name change in 1982 did not reflect a change in the definition of behavior, however. The theory of interaction was elaborated in the early 1980s by Warren Lamb's partner, Pamela Ramsden. Again, this was a refinement of the existing framework but not a change at the theoretical level. However, Ramsden herself also revised the whole interpretive framework in the early 1990s. This was a significant alteration that was unacceptable to Lamb for theoretical reasons. Therefore, from 1992 onward, Lamb has called his work, which utilizes the original interpretive framework, "Movement Pattern Analysis." Other assessment work done today under the moniker "Action Profile" uses the Ramsden framework. For more on this matter, see Eden Davies, *Beyond Dance* (London: Brechin Books, 2001), 120–127.

16. Lamb, "Development of Movement Pattern Analysis."

17. See, "New Discoveries about Interaction Revealed," *Action News* [Warren Lamb Associates newsletter], Winter 1980.

18. Carol-Lynne Moore, *Executives in Action* (London: Pitman, 1982), 19.

19. Pamela Ramsden, *Top Team Planning* (London: Associated Business Programmes, 1973), 195.

20. These figures were reported in promotional materials prepared by Lamb's consulting firm in the early 1990s.

21. Client companies have included American Express, Bank of America, Bank of England, British Gas, British Petroleum, CIGA Hotels, Colgate Palmolive, General Electric, Harrods, Heineken, Hewlett Packard, Hoover, IBM, Philips BV, Mars Confections, Monsanto, National Coal Board, Perivale Gutemann, and Saatchi & Saatchi. Moreover, Albany International, Associated Biscuits Europe, Faithful Overalls, J. Evershead and Company, London Linen Supply, and Trebor are enterprises that have utilized Movement Pattern Analysis for more than two decades.

22. In addition to over 100 articles, Lamb has written *Posture and Gesture* (London: Duckworth, 1965); *Management Behaviour*, co-authored with David Turner (London: Duckworth, 1969); and *Body Code,* co-authored with Elizabeth Watson (London: Routledge, 1979). Other treatises on Lamb's work have been written by Pamela Ramsden, *Top Team Planning* (London: Associated Business Programmes, 1973); Carol-Lynne Moore, *Executives in Action* (London: Pitman, 1982); and Eden Davies, *Beyond Dance* (London: Brechin Books, 2001). References to Lamb's work appear in a number of sources, including *The Illustrated Encyclopedia of Body-Mind Disciplines,* ed. Nancy Allison (New York: Rosen, 1999) and Gordon R. Wainwright, *Body Language* (London: Hodder & Stoughton, 2003).

23. Currently, Motus Humanus, a professional organization for movement specialists based in Denver, Colorado, certifies Movement Pattern Analysts when they have completed advanced training. Certification of professional qualification is handled through a process of examination and independent review of work done during training. For further information on this process, see the Motus Humanus web site, http://motushumanus.org.

24. Validation studies were initially carried out by Pamela Ramsden in the early 1970s. These are reported in her book *Top Team Planning.* Further studies were conducted by Dr. Deborah DuNann Winter in the mid-1980s. These are reported in Eden Davies, *Beyond Dance.* Observational reliability was tested by Dr. Martha Davis in a large study run under the sponsorship of the Laban/Bartenieff Institute of Movement Studies (New York) in the early 1980s. Among certified Movement Pattern Analysts today interobserver agreement exercises take place on a regular basis.

25. This opinion was expressed, in an interview with the author, by the retired CEO of a major international corporation that had utilized Movement Pattern Analysis in its divisions around the world for over twenty-five years. While Lamb's advice about people was valued, this manager admitted that it was hard to believe that movement study could provide such depth of insight into behavior.

4 ELEMENTS OF HUMAN MOVEMENT

Movement as a Psychophysical Event

Our bodies are constantly in motion. Even in moments of relative quietude, as when lost in thought or while sleeping, we breathe, our hearts beat, the blood courses through our veins, glandular and digestive juices flow, and the nerves continue to relay messages. These types of bodily motions proceed automatically, largely without our conscious intervention or awareness. Yet our physical well-being rests on the patterned and coordinated nature of these involuntary motions.

Of greater significance psychologically are the movements we do voluntarily. Does my neck ache from crouching over the computer? I can stretch and shift positions. Am I thirsty? I can reach for a glass of water. Am I feeling threatened? I can raise my shoulders to fend off a real or imagined blow. Is my daughter crying? I can scoop her up in a comforting embrace. As the pioneering movement educator Mabel Ellsworth Todd observes, "For every stimulus, there is a motor response," for every thought and feeling, a muscular change.[1] In this sense, voluntary human movement is always a psychophysical event, a balancing act between the material forces in the environment and the nonmaterial yet equally real influences that come from within. This has led Alexandra and Roger Pierce to comment that, "All human movement is expressive; it expresses intention."[2] Rudolf Laban puts it even more simply when he notes that, "Man moves in order to satisfy a need."[3]

Yet, to say that voluntary movements are expressive and intentional is not to conclude that we are always fully conscious of their manner of execution. Quite the contrary! Much of what we do with our bodies throughout the waking day is habitual and seemingly spontaneous. We do not have to overtax our brains to brush our teeth, pour the coffee, climb in and out of the car, or gesture while we visit with a friend. These well-practiced actions have become routine, and require only our subsidiary awareness.[4]

The tendency for voluntary motion to disappear from the center of conscious attention is increased by the fact that movement itself is ephemeral; it vanishes even as it is occurring. Movement is not stillness; it is what exists between stillnesses. And what exists between stillnesses is nothing but flux and fluid change.

The French philosopher Henri Bergson explained the nature of movement flux in the following way. Imagine you hold your hand at point A, then move it to point B. The movement of your hand traverses the distance between A and B, creating a hypothetical line in space. This line, consisting of an infinite number of points, could be infinitely divisible. But the movement itself is indivisible. Of course, we could stop the action of the arm somewhere between A and B. But then we would have two movements, not one. The essence of the movement, and our felt experience of it, is one of the indivisible continuity of change.[5]

While we experience movement as indivisible change, Bergson pointed out that we tend to *think* about movement as a series of positions. The mind works rather like a time-lapse camera, taking intermittent snapshots of the continuous flow of movement. By so doing, we reconstitute movement "as though it were made of immobilities."[6] Yet, there must be something else to movement, for, as Laban notes, "The sum of such snapshots is not yet the flux itself."[7]

The tendency of the mind to cut the flow of movement into still snapshots that form a line in time misrepresents the reality of change. Nevertheless, Bergson insists that this serves a purpose: "The breaking up of change into states enables us to act upon things."[8] Similarly, the breaking up of the indivisible flux of movement into component parts helps us to understand movement. It provides a means for "analyzing the characteristics of the whole flux."[9]

While acknowledging that human movements are ephemeral, indivisible processes of flowing change, it is nevertheless possible to gain insight into movement by breaking apart this process. Every movement involves three changing elements: there must be some activation of the body and its parts, some effort or expenditure of energy, and some motion through space. In the following sections of this chapter, the corporeal, dynamic, and spatial aspects of movement are discussed. This discussion utilizes the analytical framework developed by Rudolf Laban and refined by Warren Lamb.

In Chapter 5, this delineation of movement elements is correlated with the decision-making framework introduced in Chapter 3. Thus Chapters 4 and 5 are linked. Chapter 4 provides a foundation for understanding movement through analysis. Chapter 5 demonstrates how the analysis of movement patterns provides insight into characteristic patterns of decision-making behavior.

Effort: "The Flow of Weight in Time and Space"

Laban characterized movement as "the flow of weight in time and space."[10] The process of activating the body to change its position in space requires the exertion of physical and mental energy. Laban called this exertion "effort." In Laban's view, the energy required to move consists of four "motion factors": flow, weight, time, and space. These motion factors can be described as follows:

Flow is the relative degree of control in a movement.

Weight is the degree of pressure or force that is exerted.

Time is the changing pace of an action.

Space is the manner in which the motion is aimed and oriented.

Everything in Opposites. Each of these motion factors addresses an aspect of movement change. Thus the effort or energy used to move will vary. Laban characterized this dynamic variation as a fluctuation between contrasting qualities.

The relative degree of control in a movement, the *flow* factor, varies between the qualities of binding and freeing. Binding the flow results in a controlled or even tense action, one that can be readily arrested. On the other hand, freely flowing actions are relaxed, easygoing, and hard to stop immediately.

The relative amount of force in a movement, the *weight* factor, varies between the qualities of increasing and decreasing pressure. Movements performed with increasing pressure appear strong, firm, and unyielding, while actions with decreasing pressure look gentle, delicate, and resilient.

Changes in the pace of an action, the *time* factor, involve qualitative shifts between accelerating and decelerating. The time factor is not about maintaining a steady fast or slow pace, but rather about applying energy to *change* tempo. When the effort to accelerate is made, the movement appears to speed up. When the effort to decelerate is made, the action will be seen to slow down.

The effort to aim and orient an action, the *space* factor, involves qualitative variations between directing and indirecting. When an effort to direct is made, the movement proceeds to its destination in a straight and unswerving manner, as if there were only a single focus of interest. When the effort to indirect is made, an action reaches its destination in a roundabout and meandering manner, allowing the mover to scan many points of interest along the way.

In Laban's scheme, these eight effort qualities can be clustered into two groups: those that have a "fighting" or "resisting" characteristic and those that have a more "indulging" or "yielding" aspect. The chart below arranges the eight effort qualities into these two clusters and suggests simple everyday actions in which each quality might be seen.

EFFORT CHART

MOTION FACTOR	FIGHTING QUALITY	INDULGING QUALITY
FLOW	BINDING carrying a cup full of hot tea	FREEING shaking grass off a picnic blanket
WEIGHT	INCREASING PRESSURE kneading bread dough	DECREASING PRESSURE smoothing tissue paper
TIME	ACCELERATING catching a glass before it falls	DECELERATING sinking luxuriously into a warm bath
SPACE	DIRECTING throwing darts	INDIRECTING swirling icing onto a cake

From Simple to Complex. Laban's basic conceptualization of the dynamics of human motion is very parsimonious. There are only four motion factors and eight effort qualities. But these factors and qualities can be thought of as the dynamic building blocks from which more complex expressive movement sequences may be composed. Most actions employ combinations of effort qualities, multiplying the richness and nuance of movement expression. Moreover, these qualitative compounds can be arranged in an almost infinite variety of phrases and sequences.

For example, consider the action of waving to a friend. This is not a single act, but a series of motions that involves raising the arm, waving, and lowering the arm again. This series of actions may be performed in a variety of ways. One could raise the arm languidly, give a gentle and rather tentative wave, then slowly and carefully return the arm to its original position. Or one could swiftly thrust the arm upward, giving a firm, vigorous wave to attract attention, then casually let the arm drop. The series of actions is identical, yet how the actions are done conveys very different impressions. "Emotional trends are reflected in gesture, attitudes, gaits," observes modern dance pioneer Ted Shawn.[11] Pierce and Pierce concur: "The body's movements speak the person. Watch ten joggers pass by the front of your house and you will see ten different etchings of individuality."[12]

Individuality is etched, not only by what is done, but also by how it is done. Effort deals with how. Effort qualities modify the nature of an action and provide clues to the mover's intention. Intentions themselves cannot be seen, for the shift from thought to thought or mood to mood occurs in the inner domain of psychological space, which is opaque. Nevertheless, as Shawn puts it, each gesture is "expressive of something . . . a thought, an emotion, a purpose, a design, or a motive."[13] It is in this sense that normally invisible thoughts and feelings become perceptible as they assume a form in movement. Or one could say that movements are translucent wrappers for the flow of inner moods and intentions. The effort qualities color these movements, providing a pigment through which something of the mover's inner process may be seen.

Shape: The "Second Form" of the Human Body

Effort is not the only aspect of movement that is expressive. How the body shapes itself in traversing space is also revealing. These movement shapes are sometimes referred to as the "second form" of the human body. Interestingly, the person who coined this term was the great Renaissance artist Leonardo da Vinci, who may be considered one of the first movement analysts.

As Renaissance artists applied techniques of drawing in perspective to the human form, they became aware that the relative proportions of the figure appeared to change when the body was depicted in different poses. In order to cope with these problems of foreshortening, Leonardo embarked upon a "systematic investigation of those mechanical and anatomical processes by which the objective dimensions of the quietly upright body are altered."[14] In his attempts to combine a theory of human proportion with a theory of human movement, Leonardo conceived the idea of a "second form" of the human body, one that becomes "visible in the circling movement round his own center and that of his limbs round their various joints."[15]

Leonardo's scheme is still used by artists today to handle problems of foreshortening. Perhaps Laban, whose first career was in visual art, was familiar with Leonardo's technique. In any case, Laban coined his own term for these curved movement shapes; he called them "trace-forms." According to Laban, the "living architecture" created by human movements is "made up of pathways tracing shapes in space, and these we may call 'trace-forms.' "[16]

Warren Lamb suggests that one way to conceive these movement traces is to imagine that the joints of the body emit vapor trails, like those left in the sky by jet engines. Lamb and co-author, Elizabeth Watson, go on to assert that "although the trails criss-cross and seem muddled at first, they create an individual and distinctive shape."[17] In order to decipher this individual pattern, however, it is necessary to transform the emptiness of space into a place with some sort of landmarks. Here is how Laban and Lamb have done this.

First, Laban suggested that human movement be conceptualized as taking place within a sphere of territory. He called this territory the "kinesphere" and defined it as "the sphere around the body whose periphery can be reached by easily extended limbs" without taking a step.[18]

Once this general locale for movement was established, Laban created a geography of imaginary lines and coordinates. These lines are analogous to the lines of longitude and latitude. Just as longitude and latitude facilitate navigating on the earth's surface, so too the imaginary lines of the kinesphere provide a way to situate movement and describe the locations of trace-forms.

Laban experimented with a variety of kinespheric geographies, but Lamb has settled on a planar scheme for capturing the curves of human movement. In this scheme, three rectangular planes intersect in the center of the kinesphere. These planes correspond to the cardinal dimensions of height, width, and depth. The vertical plane stands like a door, separating the space in front of the mover from the space behind the mover. The horizontal plane is suspended like a table, separating the space above the mover's waist from the space below. The sagittal plane is extended like a rectangular wheel, separating the space to the right of the mover from the space to the left.

The point of intersection of these three planes marks the center of the kinesphere. This center point also corresponds to the center of the mover's body. This isomorphism provides a simple way to describe the shape of the "second form" of the human body. It will be recalled that Leonardo conceived this form as a series of circles traced around the body's center or around various limbs. These curved paths can be conceived to lie primarily in one or the other of these cardinal planes. This scheme allows the complex crisscrossing of the vapor trails left by movement to be unmuddled, so that a distinctive individual pattern can be perceived.

Everything in Opposites Once Again. The curved trace-forms that make up the living architecture of human movement, or the so-called "second form" of the body, reflect changes of spatial location within the three cardinal planes. Again, Laban and Lamb have characterized these changes as fluctuations between contrasting shapes.

Changes of shape in the vertical plane vary between descending and rising movements. Descending movements swerve downward and sideward, as if slanting or settling toward a lower corner of the door plane. Rising movements curve upward and sideward, veering toward the high corners of the door plane with a "tilting and tipping quality."[19]

Changes of shape in the horizontal plane vary between enclosing and spreading. Enclosing movements sweep in front and across the body, as if one were gathering in pieces of a puzzle scattered on a tabletop. Spreading movements reverse this process, creating curved paths that advance and open, as if one wanted to sweep away crumbs on a table, broadly scattering them in all directions.

Changes of shape in the sagittal plane vary between retreating and advancing. Retreating movements curl backward, with a "withdrawing, retiring quality."[20] Advancing movements project forward, as if the mover is being propelled onward.

In Lamb's scheme, these shaping processes can be clustered into two groups: those that have a concave characteristic and those that are predominantly convex. The chart (page 63) arranges the six shaping processes into these two clusters and suggests simple everyday actions in which these planar trace-forms might occur.

SHAPE CHART

PLANE OF MOTION	CONCAVE SHAPE CHANGE	CONVEX SHAPE CHANGE
VERTICAL	DESCENDING bending downward and sideward to grasp a suitcase	RISING leaning out a train window to wave good-bye
HORIZONTAL	ENCLOSING embracing a basketful of laundry	SPREADING sprawling in a comfortable chair
SAGITTAL	RETREATING snatching a small child away from a busy street	ADVANCING springing across the finish line

Positioning Oneself. In describing the shape of trace-forms, Laban observed that when we lift an arm, we trace a form resembling the shape of an opening fan. But there is a difference between the opening of the fan and the arm movement. In the case of the fan, its ribs are still visible once the opening movement is completed, "while the arm in its final positon is, for our eyes, the only remaining part of the movement."[21]

Such bodily positions are expressive. "Guilt, craft, vision, meanness, ecstasy, and lure appear in certain arrangements of arms, hands, shoulders, neck, head, and legs," Todd affirms. "Thus the stuff of the ages goes into man's thinking, is interpreted and comes out in movement and posture again."[22] The French sculptor Auguste Rodin agrees: "The form and the attitude of a human being reveal the emotions of its soul."[23] But Rodin goes on to note that positions, though expressive, have their limitations: "They never represent more than a single phase of an action."[24]

This same limitation applies to contemporary treatises on "body language" that attach great significance to momentarily held positions. There is sufficient research to suggest that poses do have meaning.[25] Nevertheless, emphasis on these moments of stillness overlooks the fact that "in the 'moving picture' lies hidden a tremendously enhanced expression of human will and feeling."[26]

The difficulty lies in capturing this "moving picture," for the fanlike trace-forms of movement can be quite complex. Shaping processes, like effort qualities, can be combined. In lifting the arm to wave, one could merely raise the arm upward and sideward, creating a rising shape in the door plane. Or one could swing the arm upward on an angle, combining rising and spreading with advancing. The waving motion and the dropping of the arm would introduce other processes of shape change. As with effort, shaping compounds can be arranged in an almost infinite variety of phrases and sequences. Yet through careful observation, individual patterns will be seen to emerge. Shape, as well as effort, reveals an "etching of individuality." Lamb asserts,

> Some people will be observed with a walk which is Shaped mainly side to side within a vertical plane—they are often difficult to overtake on a narrow pavement. Others Shape themselves predominantly along a horizontal plane—these are the people whose elbows splay out and who keep brushing you when walking alongsides. Others again will be observed to align themselves within a sagittal plane, looking rather as though they had been shot into their walk from an "on your marks, get set, Go!" position.[27]

Although the eye remembers the ending position of a movement most readily, it is the shaping process, with all its intermediate stages, that is most indicative of individual style.

The Articulate Body

It has become a cliché to observe that "the body never lies." While the body is always expressive, it is not necessarily the case that what is being expressed is the whole truth and nothing but the truth. Most of us engage in at least some form of "image management." As Robert Park, a sociologist, observed, "Everyone is always and everywhere, more or less consciously, playing a role."[28] The philosopher William James made a similar comment: "We do not show ourselves to our children as to our club companions, to our customers as to the laborers we employ, to our own masters and employers as to our intimate friends."[29] As psychologist Albert Scheflen puts it, each person has a complex personality and "a large repertoire of possible performances."[30] Thus we are able to embody a variety of social roles and to control, at least to some degree, the kind of impressions we create in our interactions with others.

This sociable image management sometimes requires creating false impressions. As psychologist and nonverbal communication specialist Paul Ekman points out, there are few human relationships that "do not involve deceit, or at least the possibility of it."[31] While lying is not a virtue, the intent to deceive need not be malevolent. Dissembling can be benign, as when one feigns pleasure over receiving an unattractive birthday gift or pretends to be sorry when guests who have overstayed their welcome finally depart. In this sense, getting along with others often necessitates some degree of playacting. To give a convincing performance, one must not only say the right things, but do the right things nonverbally. The body, too, must be articulate.

Research shows that individuals differ in their degree of nonverbal sensitivity and personal intelligence.[32] Nevertheless, most human beings have been schooled nonverbally from an early age in how to get along, what to say bodily, and what not to say. Expressive movements are not always individualistic or "authentic." Some movements have been learned through imitation of others and represent a socially conditioned repertoire of "normal" behavioral responses. Consequently, it is important to be able to differentiate between movements that are uniquely expressive of the individual and those that are merely conventional acts consciously employed to achieve a calculated effect.

Two broad bipolar categories provide a point of entry for differentiating bodily utterances, as illustrated in the chart below. First, we can discriminate between *stable* arrangements of the body (i.e., momentary poses and habitual postures or body attitudes) and *mobile* phrases of bodily action (i.e., gestures, and integrated movements or posture-gesture mergers). Secondly, we can differentiate poses and gestures that are *transitory* from patterns of postural alignment and integrated whole body expressions that are more *enduring*.

ARTICULATE BODY CHART

	Transitory	Enduring
Stable	Pose	Body Attitude
Mobile	Gesture	Integrated Movement

Pose. Laban observed that "stability and mobility alternate endlessly."[33] If one observes two friends in animated conversation, this fluctuating pattern becomes quite apparent. There are moments of stir, in which every muscle seems to be activated, and moments of stillness, in which the whole body temporarily "freezes" in a pose. This momentary immobility dissolves into a dynamic flow, which crystallizes again in a different position of stable repose. Over the course of the conversation a series of poses will emerge from the flow of action and disappear again. Each pose is transitory, reflecting a momentary mood that folds seamlessly into another mood as the conversation progresses.

Body Attitude. On the other hand, if we had the opportunity to observe one or the other of these friends in different circumstances, we might become aware that each has a characteristic posture that is held or maintained across various activities. For one person, it might be a slight tendency to hunch the shoulders. The other friend might be inclined to lift the rib cage slightly, thrusting it forward. These fixed configurations of the body are postural patterns of alignment that have become habitual. They are sometimes referred to as "body attitudes." Psychiatrist Judith Kestenberg defines body attitude as "the way the body is shaped, how it is aligned in space, how body parts are positioned in relation to one another and to favored positions of the whole body."[34] While body attitudes are malleable in childhood, they gradually solidify, becoming fixed and enduring patterns of alignment thought to represent the "somatic core of the body image."[35]

Gesture. If we set out to observe the bodily utterances of a person moving, that is, not in a state of stillness but performing some action, these motions will fall into two broad categories, Lamb asserts. We will detect some actions that are confined to one part of the body, while other movements involve the whole body in a cohesive process of postural adjustment.[36]

Lamb uses the term "gesture" to refer to actions that are confined to one part of the body. Scratching one's head, wiggling one's toes, shrugging the shoulders, uncrossing one's legs, arching the upper back—the list of possible gestures is almost endless. These isolated actions may be performed one at a time, or in simultaneous and overlapping phrases. A good example of the latter is the one-man band, whose gestural virtuosity allows him to play several instruments at the same time. But one need not be a virtuoso to gesture. As Lamb avers, "It is right and natural that hundreds of everyday actions should be confined to parts of the body alone."[37] Many such mundane actions simply do not require whole body involvement. However, Lamb cautions, if isolated motions are allowed to predominate, a puppetlike impression will be created by the mover.

This quality of artificiality arises in part because gestures are easily acquired through imitation. Nearly all of us have caught ourselves copying the mannerisms of someone we admire. Indeed, image consultants often advocate adopting certain gestures to give the appearance of power, status, and success. But merely "making the gesture" may not be sufficiently convincing. This is because the meaning of gestures differs from culture to culture.[38] Numerous anecdotes attest to the fact that movements that are innocuous in one country can be interpreted as insulting in another. For example, nonverbal communication specialist Aaron Wolfgang reports being asked to take a photo of a group of men in Rio de Janeiro. He made the gesture with the thumb and forefinger that means "OK" in the United States. When the men immediately became angry, Wolfgang switched to the thumbs-up gesture. The men smiled and he took their picture. Afterward he learned that the thumb and forefinger gesture has a very rude meaning in Brazil![39]

This anecdote illustrates the transitory nature of gestural movements. Because they are isolated actions, gestures are easily acquired and mastered. They do not require the same degree of coordination that performing a whole body action requires. As Wolfgang's tale illustrates, gestures can be employed intentionally and just as intentionally discarded. One sign can be easily substituted for another. Moreover, gestures do not have set or stable meanings. The significance of such isolated movements is subject to change, depending on the place and time of enactment.

Integrated Movement. Actions of the whole body necessitate a complex process of neuromuscular coordination and postural adjustment. This requires greater involvement of the mover, though not necessarily at the conscious level. Indeed, Laban comments that, "A completely voluntary movement, in which every detail is premeditated and controlled, is a very rare fulfillment."[40] In his view, voluntary actions usually fail in form, or in mood, or in both. Interestingly, Laban goes on to note that,

> People with excessively controlled movement, like bad actors, fail to communicate their intended response, and we cannot help but doubt the sincerity of their actions. Only when a part of the quality of movement is, or seems to be, unconscious do we speak of a natural or true expression.[41]

Lamb made a similar discovery by inquiring into the authenticity of movement. When a mover confined his or her actions to gestures, a doll-like, rather unnatural impression was created. However, Lamb found that "if there are frequent occasions when Gesture merges into Postural adjustment there is no feeling of artificiality."[42] In a postural adjustment, "each limb action is both seen and felt in relation to the body as a whole."[43] In order for this seamless merger between a part of the body and the whole body to occur, there must be a consistent process of change in effort dynamics or in how the body shapes itself in space. The whole body must move in a coherently integrative manner.

According to Lamb, waving to attract attention provides a good example of such coherently integrated movement. If the person waving is determined not to be overlooked, the movement will involve postural adjustment. This can arise at different points in the process of the wave. One person may start with a rising gesture of the arm that leads to "an upward stretch of the whole body."[44] Another person "may confine the arm raising to Gesture then involve Posture with the first quick action of waving."[45]

There are many different possibilities. But Lamb has found that by attending to the way in which adults perform posturally integrated movements, a distinctive pattern of effort and shape change can be detected. Moreover, this pattern of mobile, whole body change is authentic and enduring.

Form and Mood Go Together

How the body shapes itself in space gives form to a movement. The kind of effort involved in this kinetic shaping conveys the mover's mood and intentions. Body, shape, and effort are "inextricably interrelated," Irmgard Bartenieff writes.[46] Laban concurs, noting that, "The conventional idea of space as a phenomenon which can be separated from time and force and from expression, is completely erroneous."[47]

Based upon observations of working actions, Laban hypothesized that, "The body and its limbs are able to execute certain dynamic nuances in movement toward certain areas in space better than toward others."[48] For example, variations in pressure tend to happen in the vertical plane. Variations in focus are likely to occur in the horizontal plane. Variations in pace tend to take place in the sagittal plane. Moreover, concave shapes support fighting effort qualities, while convex shapes tend to go with indulging effort qualities.

Laban maintained that, "Movement of any dynamic shade can be made into any desired direction."[49] Nevertheless, the following correlations of effort and shape can be detected in complex actions in which the appropriate use of energy must be combined with the right spatial trajectory in order to accomplish the task. Under these circumstances, the following effort qualities and shaping processes tend to go together.

AFFINITIES CHART

	EFFORT QUALITY	SHAPING PROCESS	
(fighting) (indulging)	WEIGHT VARIATION Increasing Pressure ←——→ Decreasing Pressure ←——→	VERTICAL PLANE Descending Rising	(concave) (convex)
(fighting) (indulging)	SPACE VARIATION Directing ←——→ Indirecting ←——→	HORIZONTAL PLANE Enclosing Spreading	(concave) (convex)
(fighting) (indulging)	TIME VARIATION Accelerating ←——→ Decelerating ←——→	SAGITTAL PLANE Retreating Advancing	(concave) (convex)

These prototypic pairings complement one another. Their natural "togetherness" suggests an affinity or mutual attraction, which Laban characterizes as an aspect of movement harmony. As he elucidates, "This simplified scheme forms the basis for certain correlations of dynamic nuances with spatial directions and this reciprocal relationship rules harmonious movement in the kinesphere."[50]

Harmony, as Laban conceives it, should not be thought of in terms of what is pleasing. Rather, as in music, harmony in movement deals with deeper structural relationships that can result in dissonance as well as consonance. Since "movements of any dynamic shade can be made into any desired direction," it is also possible to combine mood and form to create a clashing pattern. Such prototypic discords are charted on the next page.

DISCORD CHART

	EFFORT QUALITY	SHAPING PROCESS	
(fighting) (indulging)	WEIGHT VARIATION Increasing Pressure ⟷ Decreasing Pressure ⟷	VERTICAL PLANE Rising Descending	(convex) (concave)
(fighting) (indulging)	SPACE VARIATION Directing ⟷ Indirecting ⟷	HORIZONTAL PLANE Spreading Enclosing	(convex) (concave)
(fighting) (indulging)	TIME VARIATION Accelerating ⟷ Decelerating ⟷	SAGITTAL PLANE Advancing Retreating	(convex) (concave)

Dynamism

Effort qualities and shaping processes belong to different domains of movement experience. Consequently, Laban looked at the interplay between effort and shape as influencing *movement harmony*; that is, how mood and form combine to create consonance and dissonance. On the other hand, elements from the same domain may be combined. For example, two or more effort elements may be simultaneously activated in an integrated movement. Or two or more shape changes can occur together. Lamb has found that a synchronous activation of movement qualities from the *same* domain affects the intensity of an action, or what he terms *movement dynamism*.

Effort Dynamism. If an exertion involves only decreasing pressure, the movement has limited intensity. It is as if one hears only a solo clarinet. But if a mover combines decreasing pressure with directing, the movement becomes richer and more intense, as if a saxophone had joined its voice to that of the clarinet. If even more energy is applied to combine decreasing pressure and directing with decelerating, the resulting dynamism of the "gliding" movement is analogous to the vigorous richness of tone achieved when clarinet, saxophone, and trumpet all play together.

Shape Dynamism. Similarly, the simultaneous activation of two or more shaping processes affects the intensity of an action. Spatial trajectories also have a dynamic character. When a shaping action is confined to a single plane, as in a simple rising, it is relatively easy to maintain balance. Such a movement has little intensity and the dynamism of the form is like that of the solo clarinet. But when shaping processes are combined, as in a motion that rises and advances, more oblique trajectories are traced. It is far less easy to balance along these tilted inclinations. The mover cannot rest but must fly or fall, and this greater instability is more dynamic. The combined tensions of the shaping process add three-dimensional volume to the movement, increasing its intensity.

Thus the dynamism of an action is directly proportional to its effort and shape loading. When a solitary effort or shape change occurs, it is as if the bodily orchestra makes only an "occasional bleep," Warren Lamb and co-author, David Turner, explain.[51] In this instance, the movement will appear to be only mildly energetic. But when several efforts change simultaneously, or when shaping processes combine to create oblique curves and volumes, it is as if all the instruments of the orchestra are "going full blast."[52] On these occasions, the resulting movements will be felt to have a lot of dynamic drive.

Everything Flows

"The sole actuality of nature resides in change," remarks architect and artist Peter Stevens. "All things are becoming. All things are flowing."[53] Because it is the quintessence of change, movement naturally flows. Flow is "going-ness." It is the kinetic current that sustains the continuity of movement. This lively continuity streams from two sources: the "dynamosphere" of effort changes and the kinesphere of shape changes. Consequently, Laban and Lamb have distinguished two types of flow: effort flow and shape flow.

Effort flow reflects fluctuations in the fluency of a movement. These fluctuations vary between qualities of binding and freeing, as noted earlier. Because of its emotional character, flow plays an important role in the creation of many movement moods. Flow is salient in dance, for example, and other expressive activities. However, Laban found that flow plays only a supporting role in working actions. The floating, gliding, dabbing, flicking, punching, slashing, wringing, and pressing motions that occur when manipulating tools and materials require focal awareness of the motion factors of weight, time, and space. The mover must concentrate on getting the pressure, pace, and focus right, while ongoing adjustments in flow require only subsidiary awareness. Effort flow is latent in working actions. It fluctuates quietly in the background, while the other motion factors are center stage.

Shape flow reflects fluctuations in the elasticity of the kinesphere. These fluctuations vary between shrinking and growing. This continuous flow of shape change has an organic basis. It can be related to breathing, in which a subtle flux between growing and shrinking accompanies inhaling and exhaling. Another example of shape flow is the "baby's amoebalike movements that go toward or away from the body center."[54] Such pliable changes are "still body focused; they do not yet go toward a goal in space or carve up the space around them."[55] In working actions, clear planar shaping processes are necessary if tools and materials are to be manipulated skillfully. Shape flow is latent, providing a baseline of elasticity from which planar shapes may emerge.

Thus, in the process of doing a task, effort flow and shape flow sustain kinetic fluency and three-dimensional plasticity, providing a baseline for action. Flow underlies skillful labor. But it is secondary in importance to the role played by the other effort elements and shaping processes.

Dividing the Indivisible

All movement is an indivisible flow. Yet in order to understand movement better, this flowing continuity of change can be broken into component parts. This is because in each voluntary action, a mover must apply dynamic energy to change the position of the body in space. Thus three elements—effort, shape, and body—are involved in every movement.

Laban characterized movement as the flow of weight in time and space. These four motion factors—flow, weight, time, and space—provide broad categories for describing the changing qualities of dynamic energy utilized in voluntary movement. Flow fluctuates between qualities of binding and freeing. Weight varies between increasing and decreasing pressure. Time shifts between accelerating and decelerating. And spatial focus changes between directing and indirecting. These eight qualities are the dynamic building blocks of human effort. The terms can be used as a descriptive framework for capturing *how* a movement is done. Since *how* an action is done is often as important as *what* is done, effort description can provide insight into a mover's mood and intentions.

Where movement flows in the space around the body is also significant. These curved "trace-forms" can be conceived to relate primarily to the cardinal planes of the kinesphere. Within each of these three planes, the body can outline two contrasting shapes. In the vertical plane, movements fluctuate between descending and rising. In the horizontal plane, movements veer between enclosing and spreading. And in the sagittal plane, trace-forms vary between retreating and advancing. Careful observation of how the body shapes itself in space reveals a distinctive pattern in which an etching of individuality may be perceived.

The interplay of body parts in stillness and in motion can be quite expressive as well. Four broad categories have been detailed: poses, body attitudes, gestures, and integrated movements. Poses and body attitudes refer to how the body arranges itself in a still position or fixed pattern of alignment. Poses are transitory, while an individual's body attitude is more enduring. Gestures are isolated actions of the body. These actions are easy to imitate and tend to be conditioned by the social and cultural environment. Integrated movements are cohesive actions in which a gesture is supported by postural adjustment through the body as a whole. The integration of part into whole is achieved through the coherent change in effort quality or shaping process. These movement patterns are not easy to imitate. Consequently, integrated movements tend to be more enduring and individualistic than gestures.

Effort, shape, and body usage are inextricably interrelated. However, differing patterns of relationship between elements may be discerned. These patterns influence the perceived harmony, dynamism, and flow of an action. For example, certain effort qualities and shaping processes are complementary, while other effort-shape combinations clash. These relationships impact both movement function and expression. Effort loading and shape loading contribute to the dynamism of an action. And in getting a job done or making a practical decision, effort and shape flow take a supporting role, providing the kinetic continuity that underlies effective action.

The essence of movement is change; all is in flux, nothing stands still. On the other hand, the more things change, the more they stay the same. It is said that one can never step in the same river twice. And this is both true and not true. As Stevens observes, "The new water chases out the old, but the pattern remains the same."[56] This observation also applies to human movement. Movement changes all the time. And yet, it remains the same because there is a pattern to the fluctuation that is individual and recognizable. In the next chapter we will examine what this individual pattern means in terms of decision-making style.

Endnotes

1. Mabel Ellsworth Todd, *The Thinking Body* (Brooklyn, NY: Dance Horizons, 1973), 1–2.

2. Alexandra Pierce and Roger Pierce, *Expressive Movement* (New York: Plenum Press, 1989), 15.

3. Rudolf Laban, *The Mastery of Movement* (Boston: Plays Inc., 1975), 1.

4. The concept of subsidiary awareness is drawn from the work of Michael Polanyi. In *Personal Knowledge* (Chicago: University of Chicago Press, 1962), Polanyi points out that in the skillful performance of any task, focal awareness is concentrated on the goal, while subsidiary awareness provides details regarding performance. For example, awareness of how the coffeepot handle feels in the hand is subsidiary to the focal concentration of pouring the coffee into the cup. In this sense, we are aware of a great deal of our movement behavior only subsidiarily.

5. For a lengthier discussion of the nature of movement, see Henri Bergson, *The Creative Mind* (New York: Wisdom Library, 1946), 142–158.

6. Ibid, 145.

7. Rudolf Laban, *The Language of Movement* (Boston: Plays Inc., 1974), 3.

8. Bergson, *The Creative Mind*, 146.

9. Laban, *The Language of Movement*, 4.

10. Rudolf Laban, "Space, Time, Weight, and Flow," National Resource Centre for Dance Laban Archive, ref. no. E(L)/5/71.

11. Ted Shawn, *Every Little Movement* (Brooklyn, N.Y: Dance Horizons, 1974), 31.

12. Pierce and Pierce, *Expressive Movement*, 14.

13. Shawn, *Every Little Movement*, 31.

14. Edwin Panofsky, *The Codex Huygens and Leonardo da Vinci's Art Theory* (Westport, CT: Greenwood Press, 1971), 125.

15. "Human Proportion," 870–874, in *The Dictionary of Art*, ed. J. Turner (London: Macmillan, 1996), 874.

16. Laban, *The Language of Movement*, 5.

17. Warren Lamb and Elizabeth Watson, *Body Code* (London: Routledge & Kegan Paul, 1979), 50.

18. Laban, *The Language of Movement*, 10.

19. Carol-Lynne Moore, *Executives in Action* (London: Pitman, 1982), 72.

20. Ibid., 74.

21. Laban, *The Language of Movement*, 46.

22. Todd, *The Thinking Body*, 2.

23. Auguste Rodin, *Rodin on Art and Artists* (New York: Dover Publications, 1983), 70.

24. Ibid., 69.

25. See, for example, Flora Davis, *Inside Intuition* (New York: New American Library, 1975), Chapter 11, and Julius Fast, *Body Language* (New York: Pocket Books, 1977), Chapter 8.

26. Rudolf Laban, *A Life for Dance*, trans. Lisa Ullmann (New York: Theatre Arts Books, 1975), 11.

27. Warren Lamb, *Posture and Gesture* (London: Gerald Duckworth, 1965), 26.

28. Robert Park, quoted in Erving Goffmann, *The Presentation of Self in Everyday Life* (Garden City, NY: Doubleday, 1959), 19.

29. William James, quoted in Goffmann, *Presentation of Self*, 48.

30. Albert Scheflen, *Body Language and Social Order* (Englewood Cliffs, NJ: Prentice-Hall, 1972), 126.

31. Paul Ekman, *Telling Lies* (New York: W. W. Norton, 1985), 23.

32. See, for example, Robert Rosenthal et al., *Sensitivity to Nonverbal Communication* (Baltimore: Johns Hopkins Press, 1979), and Howard Gardner, *Frames of Mind* (New York: Basic Books, 1985).

33. Laban, *The Language of Movement*, 94.

34. Judith Kestenberg, quoted in Irmgard Bartenieff with Dori Lewis, *Body Movement* (New York: Gordon and Breach, 1980), 111.

35. Ibid.

36. Lamb, *Posture and Gesture*, 14

37. Ibid., 31.

38. See, for example, Robert Axtell, *Gestures* (New York: John Wiley & Sons, 1991), and Desmond Morris, *Manwatching* (New York: Harry Abrams, 1977).

39. Aaron Wolfgang, *Everybody's Guide to People Watching* (Yarmouth, ME: Intercultural Press, 1995), 19–20.

40. Laban, *The Language Movement*, 49.

41. Ibid.

42. Lamb, *Posture and Gesture*, 32.

43. Ibid., 31.

44. Lamb and Watson, *Body Code*, 86.

45. Lamb, *Posture and Gesture*, 32.

46. Bartenieff with Lewis, *Body Movement*, 85.

47. Laban, *The Language of Movement*, 67.

48. Ibid., 30.

49. Ibid., 31.

50. Ibid.

51. Warren Lamb and David Turner, *Management Behaviour* (London: Gerald Duckworth, 1969), 49.

52. Ibid.

53. Peter Stevens, *Patterns in Nature* (New York: Little, Brown, 1977), 53.

54. Bartenieff with Lewis, *Body Movement*, 85.

55. Ibid.

56. Stevens, *Patterns in Nature*, 53.

5 MOVEMENT AND MAKING DECISIONS

Reconsidering the Mind and Body

"I think, therefore I am," wrote René Descartes in 1637. By so saying, the French philosopher gave primacy to mental functions over physical ones. The ground of *being* lay in abstract thought and not in visceral experience. The nature of embodiment was of little philosophical interest, for the functioning of the body, like the functioning of any other physical object, could be effectively explained through mechanics and physics. "So effective was Descartes' placing of the body," notes the contemporary philosopher Donn Welton, that the body-mind relationship was viewed as "unproblematic"[1] for nearly 300 years. As far as philosophy was concerned, it was the mind that mattered. And the mind was an entity separate from and independent of the body.

Yet during the last 100 years, a radical revision has been taking place. The existence of a transcendental and disembodied reason, one separated from and independent of the body, has been called into question. Moreover, the body itself, once so inconsequential, has become the focus of intense scrutiny, not only in philosophy, but also in psychology, linguistics, and neuroscience. As a consequence, new views are emerging regarding the relationship of body, brain, and mind.

"Guard me from the thoughts men think in the mind alone," wrote W. B. Yeats. "He who sings a lasting song thinks in marrow bone."[2] The Irish writer's poetic intuition beautifully captures the emerging view that reason cannot be divorced from sensate experience and visceral response, from what the psychologist Eugene Gendlin has called the "felt sense" of "inner bodily awareness."[3]

As understanding of brain function increases, it is becoming clear that reasonable thought is related to feeling, and feeling is woven from bodily sensation and kinesthetic response. In actuality, conscious cognition rests upon a fluid substratum of body states that are felt and known, albeit often at the level of subliminal consciousness.[4] The neural structures through which these bodily states are experienced are linked through the sensori-motor system to the neural structures of the brain.[5] In this sense, we are *thinking bodies*. The brain draws upon bodily experiences to construct the coherent images and concepts that make it possible for us to know the world and to act upon it.

As philosopher Mark Johnson observes, "Our perceptual interactions and bodily movements within our environment" generate the "schematic structures that make it possible for us to experience, understand, and reason about our world."[6] Neurologist Antonio Damasio agrees, declaring that, "Our very organism, rather than some absolute external reality, is used as the ground reference for the constructions we make of the world around us. Our most refined thoughts and best actions use the body as a yardstick."[7]

Thoughts and feelings have been considered to be immaterial abstractions invisible to the naked eye. Yet, contemporary research suggests that thinking consists of "embodied concepts" that are constructed through the active, sensual, and physical engagement of the body with the environment. Thus, thinking rests upon bodily action, and through bodily actions thinking becomes visible. Drawing upon the taxonomy of human movement discussed previously, this chapter examines relationships between patterns of thought and patterns of movement, showing how the disciplined analysis of movement gives insight into individual decision-making processes.

Applying Energy to Shape Decisions

It will be recalled that Lamb has conceptualized decision making as a three-stage process. In the first stage, one gives Attention to the problem to be solved. In the next stage, one forms an Intention to pursue a particular course of action. And in the final stage of Commitment, one acts. The decision-making process is actually more elaborate, however. For in each of these three stages there are two complementary approaches to giving Attention, forming an Intention, and making a Commitment. The names of these complementary processes and brief descriptions of each process are reviewed in the chart on the following page (reprinted from p. 43).

The three processes in the left vertical column (i.e., Investigating, Determining, and Timing) have an assertive quality in common. In each of these processes, the mover applies his or her energy to give Attention, to form an Intention, and to implement a Commitment. It should come as no

FRAMEWORK OF MANAGEMENT INITIATIVE
THE MOTIVATION TO ACT
THE DECISION-MAKING PROCESS IN ACTION

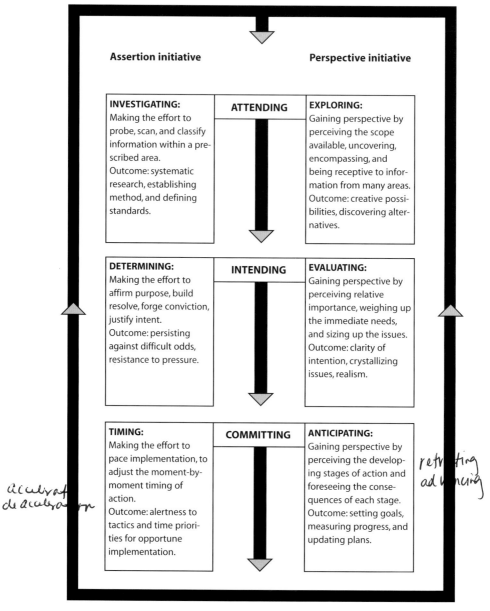

Assertion initiative　　　　　　　　**Perspective initiative**

	ATTENDING	
INVESTIGATING: Making the effort to probe, scan, and classify information within a pre-scribed area. Outcome: systematic research, establishing method, and defining standards.		**EXPLORING:** Gaining perspective by perceiving the scope available, uncovering, encompassing, and being receptive to infor-mation from many areas. Outcome: creative possi-bilities, discovering alter-natives.
DETERMINING: Making the effort to affirm purpose, build resolve, forge conviction, justify intent. Outcome: persisting against difficult odds, resistance to pressure.	**INTENDING**	**EVALUATING:** Gaining perspective by perceiving relative importance, weighing up the immediate needs, and sizing up the issues. Outcome: clarity of intention, crystallizing issues, realism.
TIMING: Making the effort to pace implementation, to adjust the moment-by-moment timing of action. Outcome: alertness to tactics and time priori-ties for opportune implementation.	**COMMITTING**	**ANTICIPATING:** Gaining perspective by perceiving the develop-ing stages of action and foreseeing the conse-quences of each stage. Outcome: setting goals, measuring progress, and updating plans.

accelerat de acelera... (handwritten)

retr...ting ad ...ncing (handwritten)

© Warren Lamb

surprise, therefore, that these processes are correlated with the variation of *effort* in bodily actions.

The three processes in the right vertical column (i.e., Exploring, Evaluating, and Anticipating) share the common aspect of creating perspective. In each of these processes, the mover positions himself or herself so as to be able to survey a wide range of information, to measure the relative importance of what is being considered, and to link new actions with those already in process. These initiatives to gain perspective are correlated with the movement processes of *shaping* in the planes.

Giving Attention Through Effort and Shape

The decision-making process begins when one becomes aware that something needs to be done. In this preliminary stage, Attention is given to the action under consideration. The two complementary approaches to giving Attention are Investigating and Exploring.

The assertive process of Investigating involves applying one's energy within a clearly defined subject area to ferret out detailed information in depth. This process requires the capacity to utilize space effort, varying the focus between directing (with its pinpointing and probing quality) and indirecting (with its scanning and scrutinizing quality).

The process of Exploring, on the other hand, involves positioning oneself so as to be receptive to a broad range of ideas and sources of information. This process requires the ability to shape in the horizontal plane, varying one's relationship to the fields of available information by enclosing (gathering in ideas from a variety of sources), and spreading (making oneself open to a range of views).

Forming an Intention Through Effort and Shape

The decision-making process progresses when one chooses one course of action from among the many possibilities under consideration. In this secondary stage, an Intention to proceed in a certain manner is formed. Two complementary approaches to forming an Intention have been delineated by Lamb—Determining and Evaluating.

The process of Determining involves applying one's energy to build the necessary resolution to act, even if the course of action chosen may prove difficult. The building of determination requires the capacity to use the weight effort, gradating the application of force by increasing pressure (becoming firm and forceful) and decreasing pressure (becoming gently persistent and resilient).

The process of Evaluating, on the other hand, involves positioning oneself so as to feel the relative value of one course of action in comparison with another. This process requires the ability to shape in the vertical plane, varying one's perspective by descending (sensing what is of little relevance) and rising (gauging what is of the greatest value).

Making a Commitment Through Effort and Shape

The decision-making process comes to fruition when one implements action. In this final stage, one no longer lingers on the threshold, considering options or intending to do something someday. Rather, one steps boldly beyond the point of no return. Again, Lamb has identified two complementary approaches to making a Commitment—Timing and Anticipating.

The process of Timing involves applying one's energy to implement the action at the right moment. This process demands the capacity to use Time effort, varying the pace of implementation adroitly by accelerating (speeding up the action) or decelerating (delaying and slowing down the pace of activity).

The process of Anticipating involves positioning oneself strategically, so that actions link and develop to achieve the desired outcomes. This requires the ability to shape in the sagittal plane, controlling the deployment of action by retreating (temporarily withdrawing for strategic reasons) and advancing (progressing when an avenue for forward motion becomes open).

Individual Decision-making Style

Everyone gives Attention, forms Intentions, and makes Commitments. Over time, however, an individual pattern can be seen to emerge. For example, one person may concentrate a great deal of time and energy at the Attention stage, with less emphasis on Intention and Commitment. This person, schematically represented in Profile A, will need to feel that all channels of information have been thoroughly researched before he or she is ready to risk acting. Another person will want to be where the action is as much as possible, concentrating on Commitment without giving much consideration to the processes of Attending and Intending. This person, as shown in Profile B, will be a risk taker, ready to seize all opportunities for action indiscriminately. Someone else may emphasize the process of Intending, taking a lot of time to build up a case and to back it up with conviction. This person, as indicated

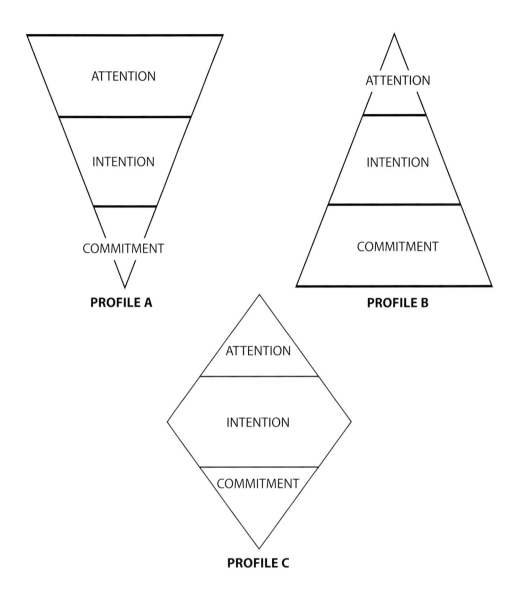

in Profile C, will be unwilling to act until completely convinced that the purpose of the action is clear and the course of action genuinely valuable.

Thus, over time, each of us reveals preferences for some stages of decision making over others. That is, we all apply effort to shape our decisions in characteristic ways. This kind of embodied thought is visible in the way we move. It can be discerned in the relative proportions of the different effort qualities and shaping processes that define our individual movement styles.

DECISION-MAKING PROCESS

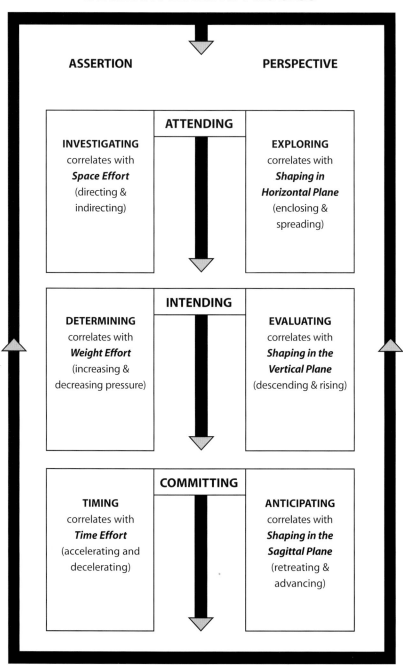

ASSERTION   PERSPECTIVE

ATTENDING

INVESTIGATING
correlates with
Space Effort
(directing &
indirecting)

EXPLORING
correlates with
*Shaping in
Horizontal Plane*
(enclosing &
spreading)

INTENDING

DETERMINING
correlates with
Weight Effort
(increasing &
decreasing pressure)

EVALUATING
correlates with
*Shaping in the
Vertical Plane*
(descending & rising)

COMMITTING

TIMING
correlates with
Time Effort
(accelerating and
decelerating)

ANTICIPATING
correlates with
*Shaping in the
Sagittal Plane*
(retreating &
advancing)

For example, the Attention-oriented individual (Profile A) will emphasize space effort and shaping in the horizontal plane in his or her movements. The Committer (Profile B) will show lots of variations in time effort and shaping in the sagittal plane. The Intender (Profile C) will stress weight effort and the movements in the vertical plane. These correlations of movement elements with decision-making processes are shown on page 84.

Normal adults will employ all the effort qualities and all the shaping processes in their movements. But they will not do so evenhandedly. Some effort qualities will be emphasized while others are barely present. Certain shaping processes will be quite evident, while some are moderate, and others are very minimal. These movement patterns can be discerned over time through disciplined observation and analysis.

While it is true that the essence of movement is change, it is equally true that the more things change, the more they stay the same. Hidden within the fluctuating dynamics, the ephemeral interplay of body parts, and the shifting trace-forms of spatial change, there is an ordered pattern. Movement is both habitual and individual. Each person has a characteristic way of using the body, applying effort, and tracing shapes. The individual may be unaware of these habitual patterns. But other people will recognize them, for these repeated nonverbal behaviors are as characteristic as the sound of a voice or the shape of facial features. It is this proportional pattern of effort and shape emphases that reveals an individual's characteristic approach to decision making.

The Significance of Integrated Movement

In studying individual movement style in relation to decision-making processes, it is necessary to distinguish movements that are both unique and enduringly characteristic from fleeting actions that are calculated to give a certain impression. The degree of bodily involvement has proven to be the key to unlocking what is authentically expressive of the individual. Poses, which are fleeting, and gestures, which activate only a part of the body, can be assumed at will. These kinds of movements are subject to a certain amount of conscious manipulation. While undoubtedly meaningful in some contexts, poses and gestures do not reveal individual decision-making style. But, as discussed in Chapters 3 and 4, integrated movements do.

The consistency of effort or shape change in an integrated movement conveys an impression of coherence and authenticity. When the whole body is involved, the whole person is involved. Moreover, while there are only a handful of effort qualities and shaping processes, these can be combined and phrased in thousands of variations that are uniquely individual. As Todd noted,

> A causal world over-emphasizes the face. Memory likes to recall the whole body. It is not our parents' faces that come back to us, but their bodies, in the accustomed chairs, eating, sewing, smoking, doing all the familiar things. We remember each as a body in action.[8]

It is the pattern of the whole body in action that is most characteristic of the individual. Thus Movement Pattern Analysis is based upon the coherent effort and shape qualities that are integrated in whole body actions. These are the patterns that reveal individual decision-making style.

Movement Harmony and Interaction Style

When assessing a person's decision-making pattern, the incidences of space, weight, and time qualities are recorded through disciplined observation. The instances of shaping movements in the horizontal, vertical, and sagittal planes are also noted. In this way, the relative proportion of each assertion and perspective can be calculated. The interaction style is also derived from these effort and shape observations.

As noted previously, Lamb has discerned four different interaction styles: *sharing*, *private*, *neutral*, and *versatile*. Each of these styles draws upon Laban's harmonic theory of the affinity of effort and shape. Laban hypothesized that certain effort qualities are executed more easily toward certain areas of space. For example, directing often occurs with an enclosing shape, increasing pressure with a descending movement, and accelerating with a backward retreating action. These prototypic pairings were considered by Laban to rule "harmonious movement in the kinesphere."[9] By extension, dissonance results from a mismatching of effort and shape. Lamb has found Laban's theory of the harmony of effort and shape relevant to determining interaction style.

Sharing Style

For example, in a sharing interaction style, the individual needs to carry out the processes of Attending, Intending, or Commiting with and through other people. The sharing individual wants to create a reciprocal relationship, making his or her initiatives available as well as drawing on the motivations of others. This interaction atmosphere is created nonverbally through affined pairings of effort and shape. In the sharing of Attention, for instance, the individual wants to Investigate and Explore with and through others, sharing information and brainstorming ideas. The harmonious pairing of directing with enclosing and indirecting with spreading nonverbally lets other people know that they are welcomed into this communicative process.

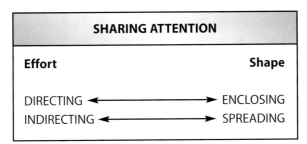

In the Intention stage, the pairing of increasing pressure with descending and decreasing pressure with rising invites others to present their views, arguing, persuading, and encouraging colleagues to come to a common position.

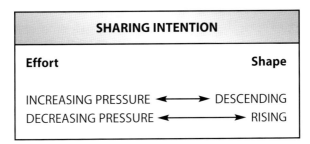

In the Commitment stage, the pairing of accelerating with retreating and decelerating with advancing creates an operational atmosphere in which everyone is able to collaborate in taking action.

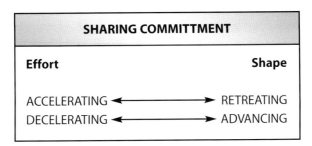

Private Style

On the other hand, with a private interaction style the individual prefers to carry out the processes of Attending, Intending, or Commiting independently. The independent person actively makes his or her initiative unavailable to others, preferring to "go it alone" rather than contributing to or drawing on the motivational input of associates. This interaction style is created nonverbally through the discordant pairings of effort and shape. The independent Attender, for example, prefers to Investigate and Explore alone. The discordant pairing of directing with spreading and indirecting with enclosing creates a nonverbal barrier that protects his or her independence.

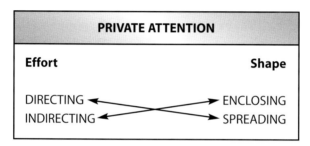

The private Intender prefers to come to grips with issues and priorities independently. The clashing combination of increasing pressure with rising and decreasing pressure with descending establishes privacy.

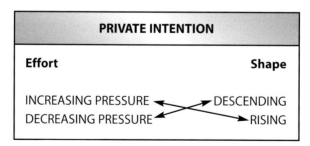

The private Committer likes to act when he or she is ready, without waiting to coordinate implementation with anyone else. Combining accelerating with advancing and decelerating with retreating in the Commitment stage creates a nonverbal atmosphere that allows the individual to act on his or her own, independently of others.

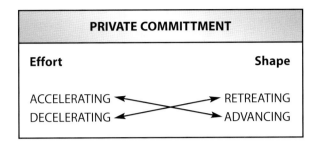

Neutral Style

With a neutral style, the individual is dependent upon the interactional initiatives of others. This style occurs when there is a significant disparity in the magnitude of assertion and perspective in a given stage of decision making. Consider Profile D, in which the proportion of Investigating is very high and the proportion of Exploring is very low. While this person has a lot of energy invested in Attending, he or she will be unable to match this energy with shape so as to structure a communicative interaction. A similar situation would result if the Exploring were much higher than the Investigating, as in Profile E. In this case, the neutral individual could create an open structure for communication but lack the energy to focus a reciprocally informative exchange. Whenever there is a substantial difference in the magnitude of assertion and perspective in Attending, Intending, or Committing, the mover will be unable to combine effort and shape either consonantly or dissonantly. The capacity to take initiative to create a sharing exchange or to establish privacy will be limited. Thus while individuals with a neutral style can adapt to the interactional needs of others, they may find it difficult to convey their own needs convincingly on the nonverbal level.

PROFILE OF NEUTRAL INTERACTION STYLE

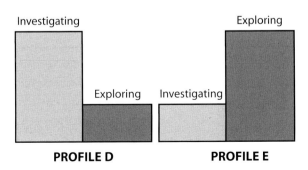

Versatile Style

Those with a versatile interaction style, on the other hand, combine a need to share with a need for independence. The versatile Attender, for example, will need to share ideas and information with others on some occasions, and at other times will prefer to give attention privately. A relative equality in the magnitude of assertion and perspective often results in a versatile style. For example, a versatile Attender will likely have a rich movement repertoire of directing, indirecting, enclosing, and spreading. This allows the versatile Attender to embody both consonant and dissonant combinations of effort and shape. Versatility at any stage of the decision-making process permits the individual to turn on the stream of interaction and to turn it off—without saying a word.

The interrelationship of effort qualities and shaping processes can be different at each stage of decision making. Thus it is not uncommon to find an individual who shares Attention, is neutral regarding his or her Intentions, and prefers to act independently at the point of Commitment. While the harmonic theory of effort and shape affinities appears simple at first glance, the resulting behavioral variations are rich and complex.

Overall Factors

Dynamism

Dynamism is the number of simultaneous novel or non-routine cycles of decision making an individual will initiate and continue. Some individuals like to see a decision-making process through to its conclusion before starting another process. At this lower level of dynamism, the person will tend to sequence projects, finishing one before taking on another. Other people thrive on having multiple projects going at the same time. These individuals prefer to be Attending, Intending, and Committing simultaneously. At this higher level of dynamism, the person will tend to overlap projects, keeping many different decision-making processes going at the same time.

This relative difference in dynamism is related to the effort and shape "loading" in an individual's movement style. When two or three effort qualities simultaneously cohere in an integrated movement, the resulting action will be more intensely energetic than a whole body action colored with only one effort quality. Similarly, when two or three shaping processes are consistently integrated in a movement, the resulting action will be more concentratedly intense than a movement in which only one shape change occurs. This effort and shape loading provides the key to assessing dynamism in decision-making style. There is a directly proportional relationship between the number of simultaneous effort and shape changes in the integrated movement pattern and the number of simultaneous nonroutine decision-making processes an individual can handle.

Identifying

Identifying, the spontaneous readiness to respond, participate, and become involved in an action, is based upon the relative amount of integrated effort flow and shape flow in an individual's movement pattern. Longitudinal movement studies of individuals from infancy to early adulthood conducted by Judith Kestenberg have revealed that effort and shape flow predominate in early childhood and gradually decrease with maturity.[10] When an adult retains a great deal of effort and shape flow variation, he also appears to retain a certain childlike spontaneity and readiness to respond. The high Identifier tends to be drawn into whatever is happening automatically, perhaps even indiscriminately. Those with a relatively lower retention of flow will tend to be more discerning and less spontaneous in response.

Putting It All Together

By carefully observing the effort qualities and shaping processes that color an individual's whole body actions, a characteristic movement pattern can be detected. From the total number of observations taken, the relative proportion of each effort factor and shaping process can be calculated as a set of percentages. Other simple calculations are used to determine the interrelationships of effort and shape and the relative degrees of dynamism and identifying. These elements of movement can then be correlated with the *Frameworks of Management Action and Interaction* (pp. 43 & 49) to represent the individual's characteristic approach to decision making.

Though not shown in full detail, the basic calculation and correlation processes are illustrated in the following two charts. The first chart, represents a hypothetical set of movement observations. This indicates that 28 of 100 movements involved variations in space effort, while 9 of 100 movements occurred in the horizontal plane, only 7 of 100 movements showed a variation in weight, and so on.

INTEGRATED MOVEMENTS OBSERVED	
EFFORT Variation	**SHAPING in Planes**
Space	**Horizontal Plane**
Directing or Indirecting **28**	Enclosing or Spreading **9**
Weight	**Vertical Plane**
Increasing Pressure or Decreasing Pressure **7**	Descending or Rising **6**
Time	**Sagittal Plane**
Accelerating or Decelerating **30**	Retreating or Advancing **20**

Because the total number of integrated movements analyzed here equals 100, the relative proportions of effort and shape elements can be easily converted to percentages. When the movement elements are correlated with the six action motivations of Investigating, Exploring, Determining, Evaluating, Timing, and Anticipating, as shown below, the relative emphases in decision-

ACTION PATTERN	
EFFORT [65%]	**PERSPECTIVE [35%]**
ATTENDING [37%]	
Investigating [28%]	Exploring [9%]
Making the effort to probe, scan, and classify information within a prescribed area. (Outcome: systematic research; establishing method; defining standards.)	Gaining perspective by perceiving the scope available, uncovering, encompassing, and being receptive to information from many areas. (Outcome: creative possibilities; discovering alternatives.)
INTENDING [13%]	
Determining [7%]	Evaluating [6%]
Making the effort to affirm purpose, build resolve, forge conviction, justify intent. (Outcome: persisting against difficult odds; resistance to pressure.)	Gaining perspective by perceiving relative importance, weighing up the immediate needs, and sizing up the issues. (Outcome: clarity of intention; crystallizing issues; realism.)
COMMITTING [50%]	
Timing [30%]	Anticipating [20%]
Making the effort to pace implementation, to adjust the moment-by-moment timing of action. (Outcome: alertness to tactics and time priorities for opportune implementation.)	Gaining perspective by perceiving the developing stages of action and foreseeing the consequences of each stage. (Outcome: setting goals; measuring progress, and updating plans.)

making style can be represented proportionally, by numerical percentages.

On the basis of these percentages, the profile can be interpreted. Any action motivation of 20 percent or more will be a significant feature in the individual's approach to decision making. Any motivation between 10 percent and 19 percent will be adequately covered. Any action motivation with a magnitude of less than 10 percent will tend to drop out of the decision-making process, or be tacked on at the end, as a kind of afterthought.

A terse interpretation of this pattern suggests that this person is highly Commitment oriented (50 percent), and that his decision-making process is likely to be driven by a need to get things done. This drive is backed up by a moderately strong Attention orientation (37 percent), with less emphasis on the Intention stage (13 percent). An individual with a profile like this is able to move flexibly from initial consideration into action. He will not waste much time worrying about whether he should or should not act. The process of judging the value of an action will most likely take place after the action has been completed. Only then will this person slow down to ask himself, "Was it worth it?"

Timing (30 percent) and Investigating (28 percent) are his predominant initiatives. This person likes to control the pace of implementation, working to schedule within a precisely defined field of information. The next initiative in order of priority is Anticipating (20 percent). This form of perspective adds a strategic dimension to the precise implementation of action, allowing the individual to foresee difficulties and to link current actions with developing trends in order to achieve his goals in a timely manner.

In the Attention stage there is an emphasis on assertion (Investigating at 28 percent) in relation to perspective (Exploring at 9 percent). There will be a tendency to set out what is to be considered quite specifically, and this may result in a premature closing of possible alternative ideas and information. This could become a problem in situations where the tried and true methods do not work and new approaches are necessary.

The relatively slight emphasis on Determining (7 percent) and Evaluating (6 percent) suggests that this individual will be able to respond rapidly to immediate needs without getting stuck at the Intention stage. But this very flexibility and responsiveness may sometimes lead him to give way when others apply pressure. He will find it difficult to stand his ground and this could become problematic, depending upon the types of pressures brought to bear on him.

Of course, a full interpretation of this profile would give much more case and point regarding each of the features mentioned above. Moreover, the generic reading of this pattern would be modified in relation to information gained from the direct interview and from other sources in the working environment. This brief description merely sketches how the movement behavior is linked to the interpretive framework to present a picture of the individual's preferred approach to decision making. The profile itself is based entirely upon the analysis of movement behavior. Making this analysis relevant to the individual or corporate client draws upon many other consulting skills.

In this sense, working with the individual or client company involves "putting it all together"—not only assessing movement behaviors and linking these to decision-making style—but also relating these patterns to the individual and corporate situation so as to facilitate a more intelligent use of human resources. In the next chapter various applications of Movement Pattern Analysis are described in greater detail and illustrated with individual and corporate case histories.

Endnotes

1. Donn Welton, ed., *The Body* (Oxford: Blackwell, 1999), 3.

2. W. B. Yeats, "The King of the Great Clock Tower."

3. Eugene Gendlin, *Focusing* (New York: Everest House, 1978), 11.

4. For an extended discussion of this phenomenon, see Antonio Damasio, *The Feeling of What Happens* (London: Vintage, 2000).

5. For a more detailed explanation of the "embodied mind," see George Lakoff and Mark Johnson, *Philosophy in the Flesh* (New York: Basic Books, 1999).

6. Mark Johnson, *The Body in the Mind* (Chicago: University of Chicago Press, 1987), 19.

7. Antonio Damasio, *Descartes' Error* (London: Papermac, 1996), xviii.

8. Mabel Ellsworth Todd, *The Thinking Body* (Brooklyn, NY: Dance Horizons, 1973), 1.

9. Rudolf Laban, *The Language of Movement* (Boston: Plays Inc., 1974), 31.

10. Judith Kestenberg and Mark Sossin, *The Role of Movement Patterns in Development* (New York: Dance Notation Bureau Press, 1979).

6 THE CASE FOR MOVEMENT STUDY

This method—or, more accurately, this science—of movement study . . . is so remarkable that at first its significance is difficult to grasp. Certainly it is not easy to explain. But if we think of human movement as we should—*as the outward and visible symbol of man entire*, his spirit mirrored indelibly in every conscious and unconscious reflex movement he makes—we have *for the first time in human history* a complete diagnosis of him which allows of no error and cannot lie.

Olive Moore[1]

These words were written in 1954 by a British journalist who was reporting on the industrial work of Laban and Lawrence. The writer overstates the case, no doubt. Nevertheless, in the five decades since these words were written, Laban-based movement study has demonstrated its efficacy in promoting understanding of self and others in the business world. This understanding has helped individuals find work that is satisfying and well suited to their capabilities. It has assisted employers in using human resources appropriately. Through the application of movement analysis, management teams have achieved a more balanced approach to decision making. And by means of the objective and non-judgmental language of the *Framework of Management Initiative*, individuals who are different have been able to collaborate more effectively, despite their contrasting management styles.

Drawing upon Movement Pattern Analysis case histories of individuals and management teams, this chapter reviews the case for movement study. The aim is to show, in practical terms, how movement analysis illuminates individual patterns of initiative and how these patterns influence decision making in the context of management teams.

Individual Assessment

Before looking at specific case studies, it is important to reiterate that the movement analysis techniques developed by Laban, Lawrence, and Lamb have always emphasized *individual* features of job performance. The original time and motion studies conducted by Taylor and the Gilbreths aimed to standardize how jobs were to be performed. In contrast, Laban and Lawrence never attempted to define "the one best way to do the job." Warren Lamb continued that tradition. Consequently, Movement Pattern Analysis (MPA) is not a standardized test. In contrast to contemporary psychological assessments, individuals are not being compared to a "normal" decision-making profile that has been derived statistically. Movement Pattern Analysis is idiographic, not nomothetic.[2] That is, Movement Pattern Analysis aims to map what is particular, distinctive, and unique to the individual. This emphasis on the significance of individual initiative profoundly affects how Movement Pattern Analysis is used in selection, placement, and career guidance. The following cases illustrate these uses.

Selection and Placement

Movement Pattern Analysis has been used to assist in the processes of selecting and placing individuals in senior management positions. It is never the sole assessment utilized, for most companies have standard hiring procedures. Candidates will be screened preliminarily to make sure that they have the necessary technical expertise and management experience. In addition, standardized psychological measures, such as intelligence and personality tests, may be used. Candidates who survive these preliminaries will be short-listed. It is at this point that Movement Pattern Analysis proves relevant. As one former chief executive confided, "I think you still have to be influenced by the personalities and needs of individuals . . . their training and background. All these factors enter into how you judge people in the jobs you are putting them in. But you can still get someone who looks like he will fit and then doesn't."[3]

This was the case with Scotcros Ltd., a British holding company. "We were faced with a difficult management relationship problem in one of our subsidiaries," recalls Alan Devereux, deputy chairman. "Something was not quite right but we were unable to identify it."[4] Warren Lamb was called in to profile the management team. The problem turned out to be the general manager. "His profile showed him to be very low on commitment,"

Devereux recounts. After being shown his profile, the general manager "agreed he found it very difficult to make decisions."[5] A reorganization of the management team was undertaken. A full year later, Devereux reported that pretax profits of the subsidiary had doubled. He credited this improvement to the changes in management brought about through the use of Movement Pattern Analysis.[6]

Of course, it is far better if the right person can be appointed from the beginning. After a decade of using Movement Pattern Analysis, Ian Marks, managing director of Trebor Ltd., reported that rates of successful appointments had significantly improved. With the additional information about candidates provided by the profile, Marks observed, "we are now wrong only about 10 percent of the time. In the old 'track record and hunch' days, it was closer to 40 percent."[7]

In addition to recruiting from outside, Trebor has also used Movement Pattern Analysis to promote from within. For example, a new group secretariat post was created. This job entailed setting up agendas for top-level management meetings and following up on decisions taken at these meetings. Decision-making requirements for this post were sketched: the manager had to be research-oriented and a good communicator.[8] Then these requirements were compared with individual profiles of more than 200 top managers in the company. On this basis, the chief chemist, Arthur Sansome was appointed. Though duties of the new job were quite different than those of his former position, Sansome was happy with the change. Moreover, according to Marks, Sansome "proved invaluable in his new post."[9] Trebor relied upon Movement Pattern Analysis in many other instances of internal recruitment. For example, a man had joined the company as a brand manager. His MPA profile showed more potential, however. And so Trebor transferred him into senior sales management and later promoted him further, naming him as Managing Director of their Indonesian subsidiary.[10]

In addition to identifying management potential, Movement Pattern Analysis can also be used to reassign executives who are found to be doing jobs for which they are unsuited. For example, the job of a production manager is to plan and program production in a timely way, so that the goods go out the factory door when they are scheduled to do so. These functions require Timing and Anticipating initiatives. In this instance, the profile of the production manager (facing page) revealed a strong Attention orientation, with little emphasis on Commitment. While this fellow was highly thought of by his managing director, "he was consistently failing to reach production targets," Pamela Ramsden reported.[11] "In fact," she recounted, "we found he had concentrated on developing highly specialized knowledge and expertise about the production process."[12] To better draw on this strength, the manager was named production adviser and reassigned to head a review of organization and methods that was much needed by the firm. This more research-oriented post matched his pattern of decision-making initiative far better, and the company benefited from the reappointment.

PROFILE OF PRODUCTION MANAGER

ATTENTION	Investigating	29%	(Very High)
	Exploring	40%	(Very High)
INTENTION	Determining	10%	(Moderate)
	Evaluating	15%	(Moderate)
COMMITMENT	Timing	2%	(Very Low)
	Anticipating	4%	(Very Low)

Career Guidance

"If a person is in a situation whose requirements he can meet through a physical application in line with the pattern of his Posture/Gesture mergings," Lamb writes, "then he will have aptitude for taking action to deal with those requirements."[13] This form of assessment based on integrated movement patterns has been applied to careers. The case histories cited in the previous section represent this application from the point of view of the employer who wants a job done effectively. The case histories discussed in this section take the point of view of the individual who either wants a satisfactory career or wants to enhance performance in the profession he or she has already chosen.

Understanding one's pattern of decision-making initiatives can be used to facilitate career development. This was reported to be the experience of Christopher Osborne, who sought Lamb's advice upon inheriting the controlling share in a small advertising company after his father's death. The company had been allowed to run down and Osborne, who was only thirty years old at the time, was not sure that he wanted to take on executive responsibility, or if he was suitable for such a role. The Movement Pattern Analysis, however, revealed that Osborne was strongly Intention oriented. Lamb identified Osborne's major strengths as "vision, firmness of purpose, and a determination to see things through"—all valuable traits for a manager who needs to turn things around.[14] Over the next six years, Osborne did just that. He restructured the company's management structure and financial policy, enabling the group to grow 10 times as big. In 1972, the *Times* reported that "there can be no doubt of Osborne's success" and cited the Osborne Group as "the third largest British-owned advertising agency."[15] Osborne himself was quoted as attributing much of this success to the advice given by Lamb on the basis of Movement Pattern Analysis of key people in the agency.[16]

In another instance, Warren Lamb was approached by a classically trained concert pianist named Ronald Meachen. "I was having trouble with my playing," Meachen recalled many years later. "My tuition at the Royal Academy was inadequate. I had been taught a particular method and I probably pursued it too much. That is why it was suggested that I do a movement course with Warren."[17]

A meeting was arranged and while the two men chatted, Lamb made notes about Meachen's movement patterns. These notes were used to assess the range of motion in terms of effort and shape elements. Based on this analysis, a course of individualized movement lessons was designed by Lamb to extend the range of physical behavior and by so doing to redress some of the technical problems affecting Meachen's musical performance.

The assessment revealed an exceptional amount of flow (very high Identifying). There was a strong emphasis on Determining, whereas the concentration of time and energy in Commitment was relatively slight. Lamb's report indicates that this was evidenced in movement phrasing as a difficulty in "achieving a convincing finality."[18] In Commitment, the approach to Timing was dominated by an over-emphasis on accelerating. Lamb's notes reflect concern about the "lopsided" range in this effort element, which expressed itself as a sort of anxious over-hastiness when Meachen was compelled to take action.[19]

Lamb also observed Meachen playing the piano. In his report to Meachen, Lamb referred to these observations, noting that Meachen maintained a "swaying attitude" but that this swaying was segregated from head movements and breathing patterns. Lamb felt this spatially constricted swaying was related to Meachen's complaint that he experienced a building up of tension while playing that left him feeling he must do something but he did not know what.[20]

Based on these observations, Lamb designed an individualized course in movement. Lamb's procedure was first to demonstrate to the individual the relative extent of the Effort and Shape ranges as shown from the analysis. Enlarged, dancelike movements were used to convey the student's preferences. Then the student was shown how these preferences colored his everyday activities—"his walk, for example, shaking hands, way of opening a door, picking up a telephone," etc.[21] Then training was undertaken to extend the student's range of effort and shape. In Meachen's case, a sequence was designed to emphasize variation in Timing (accelerating and decelerating) within a shaping process that utilized the sagittal and vertical planes. The sequence was to be repeated, with scrupulous attention to detail. Ways to incorporate elements of this sequence into everyday activities were explored. In Meachen's case, this involved specifying how he executed actions preparatory to performing, such as adjusting the height of the piano bench and signaling his readiness to begin to the orchestra conductor. The aim was to incorporate more integrated movements into these preparations so as to counteract Meachen's tendency to lapse into gesture when nervous.

Lamb gave over 100 individual development courses like this in the late 1950s and early 1960s. He reports that "Most of those who have taken this type of course have reported benefit."[22] Meachen became quite enthusiastic about the kinesthetic approach to teaching music. In an interview 46 years after the initial course, Meachen reported that he still did the exercises Lamb designed for him from time to time. He found these "useful for coordination and helping me to relax." He also reported that the exercises helped him to "not do things too hurriedly."[23] These comments suggest that the exercises designed to counteract the segregation of body actions, to minimize the tendency towards tense rigidity, and to provide more variation in timing have had favorable effect.

While Meachen observed that many other things had happened since he worked with Lamb, he concluded by saying that, "I do have the general feeling that my piano playing is much freer now. The movement may have played a role in that."[24]

Team Analysis

The Power of Pattern

In *Posture and Gesture*, Warren Lamb makes the following salient point:

> The discovery of the features that are always present in physical behaviour is significant, but it must be interpreted with care. We are not saying that individuals always behave the same in all situations. We are saying that however differently they behave, there are certain features common to their physical behaviour.[25]

The features common in physical behavior can be correlated with a pattern of decision-making initiatives. There is a power in this pattern because it is reiterated performatively day in and day out. As Ramsden notes, "If a manager has a certain degree of freedom of action and has a reasonably stable sense of identity,"[26] he or she will act in accordance with the Movement Pattern Analysis profile. This pattern of action will in turn "create a certain kind of business climate."[27] Ramsden sees this reflected in how managers describe their job situations. For example, a manager who is strong in Determining and weak in Exploring will say: "But the situation here demands persistence and determination. I recognize I don't do much *exploring* but there's never time. I would like to concentrate more on that side of things but the pressure at present is just too great."[28]

The manager who is strong in Exploring and weak in Determining in exactly the same situation will say, "Well, I never do push things much. There's no need really. There's always a way round a problem. If you once stop looking for alternatives in this kind of business you've had it."[29]

Interaction patterns also influence how a manager approaches a situation. According to Ramsden, the manager who shares Determining and Evaluating will say: "Of course in this kind of set up you have to make things clear. People don't know where they are if you don't take a firm stand. I assure you it's absolutely essential to talk straight to people, then they'll get on with it."[30]

The manager who shares Investigating and Exploring in the same situation will say: "Well I just think it's pretty important to involve people from the beginning. I always try to get my subordinates to contribute to any plan. I find you get much greater cooperation if you just talk to them on their own level and ask for suggestions. Once they're involved they tend to get on with it much better."[31]

The manager who shares Timing and Anticipating in the same situation "may pay elaborate lip service to whatever's going, but in fact he'll just get on with it. He'll just organize people into action."[32]

Understanding the individual pattern of initiative for action and interaction provides valuable information about what each manager contributes to the management team. By examining the relative strengths and weaknesses of each manager on a team, it is possible to create a composite profile of the team as a whole. This team analysis provides vital information about the types of initiatives that senior management will undertake. This has proven to be of predictive value in terms of understanding the kind of business climate a team will engender. Management teams must be proactive as well as reactive. Movement Pattern Analysis provides insight into the proactive aspects of management, as the following case studies of management teams illustrate.

Groupthink

There is some truth in the old adage that "like hires like." In Movement Pattern Analysis terms, this practice leads to a senior management team composed of individuals with similar profiles. Individual decision-making initiative is powerful because it is actively reiterated. In a team of like-minded individuals, this pattern of repeated actions has even greater impact. The strongest decision-making initiatives are reinforced while the less emphasized aspects of the decision-making process receive so little attention that they can become blind spots. The result is *groupthink*.[33]

Groupthink has been identified by social psychologists as a characteristic of overly cohesive groups. Symptoms of groupthink include overconfidence and risk taking, suppression of dissent, and collective rationalization. Groupthink biases the decision-making process and can have adverse effects on management policy and action.

Lamb has been able to simulate groupthink in management seminars by clustering individuals with similar profiles in subgroups. As Davies reports, this was done with executives from the Italian CIGA hotel group. Three groups of four managers were created. One group was composed of Attention-oriented individuals; a second of Intenders; and a third of Committers. Each group was given the same task: to report on initiatives for an improved strategy on security. The Attention group listed twenty-seven different definitions of types of security and "recommended a research group should be set up to look into the matter and report back in three months."[34] The Intention group recommended that a security manager be appointed at each hotel and clearly spelled out the nature of his or her duties and authority. They also listed points on which the group had disagreed. The Commitment group drew on matters that were already in the pipeline, advocating that the new staff training scheme include education on security and that building renovations in process incorporate security measures. This group wanted these changes to have "immediate effect."[35]

In a similar exercise, executives from the American manufacturer, Albany International, were arranged in groups and asked to report on ways "to improve inter-company transfers of personnel."[36] The Attention group considered the principles involved in moving people around the world, the impact of strange cultures, and the strain on families. They reached no conclusions and had no recommendations to make. The Intention group "declared emphatically what should and should not be done" and presented examples of transfers that "they believed would be wrong."[37] The Commitment group made "thirty three quick-fire recommendations" for steps to make transfers more acceptable.[38]

Lamb has done this sort of exercise in countless client companies. He has found that when individuals with similar profiles are given a task, they tend to define it in terms of their shared predominant decision-making initiatives. Attenders will feel that the matter needs to be given full consideration in all aspects before any concrete action can be taken. Intenders will take a stand on what should or should not be done. Committers will try to connect the new problem to whatever is already in the pipeline so as to get immediate action and quick results.

The power of the pattern of individual initiative is reinforced when the group is made up of like-minded individuals. At the subgroup level in a company, there is no inherent danger in this kind of groupthink. In fact, subgroups can be created when certain initiatives are appropriate to a particular task. However, when the entire top management team begins to develop a bias in decision making, problems can result.

Hoover is a case in point. In 1969, a strategy of diversification was announced. Hoover's intention was to move out of the domestic appliance market into new fields through acquisitions. As Lamb explains, the initiatives appropriate for acquiring companies in new fields, i.e., those in which the purchasing firm has had little experience, are Investigating and Exploring.

However, the top executives at Hoover were oriented toward Determining, Timing, and Anticipating. As Lamb illustrates,

> Basically this translates into the formula, "Let's apply our will and tactical operating flair to making the best of what we have got, setting objectives along the lines of existing trends."[39]

In short, there was a conflict between the declared strategy and the predominant motivations of the managers who were to implement it.

As a consequence, the company rejected scores of acquisition proposals. By 1974, Hoover was still locked into the domestic appliance market. "In view of the problems which then overtook the company," Lamb opined, "its executives might well have wished they had truly accomplished the diversification exercise."[40]

Lamb believes that the strength of a top executive's drive to act "in accordance with [his or her] pattern of predominant initiatives is much greater than is currently assumed."[41] For example, if a person with strong Exploring has power, he or she will "interpret, select, or perhaps distort available data to support a strategy of going into unprecedented areas."[42] The Explorer will find a way to follow his predilections, "even if colleagues offer counter-arguments" or the business climate is unfavorable.[43]

This was the case with an up-and-coming high-tech company. The enterprise had been built up by its visionary and entrepreneurial CEO, whose profile emphasized Exploring, Timing, and Anticipating (see next page). Since both Determining and Evaluating were of only slight magnitude, this manager was not inclined to sort out the pros and cons of a matter before taking action or to position himself and hold that position resolutely. Here was a person who cast around for new ideas and then swiftly moved to capitalize on them opportunistically. Dynamic, charismatic, and enthusiastic, he found it easy to carry other people along with him. In many respects, these traits had served him well and he had been successful in the fast-changing high tech environment.

However, as CEO, he had built up a top team of like-minded individuals. Virtually every senior manager was Attention and Commitment oriented. In particular, no one on the top team was strong in Evaluating. So while there was a great feeling of esprit de corps, the top executives were prone to be unrealistically over-optimistic, to take risks, and to explain away any warnings that might interfere with their exploratory committing.

Everything went fine for a while. Then the group to which the company belonged was sold to an international group. The high tech people were not happy with the new ownership, and a decision was taken to negotiate a management buyout. In order to fund the management takeover, it was necessary to raise cash by selling equity to investors. And this is where the company's exploratory commitment finally proved problematic. In the headlong rush to raise funds, there was a lack of clarity and discipline as to the sorts of agreements that were being made with investors. At the end of the day, the senior management team discovered that they had lost control of the company. The financiers of the buyout took over. Their only interest was to turn the company into a "cash cow." Pressure was put on management to make a profit, or else. Many executives were fired, others left, and those who remained suffered from the stress of working in a hostile environment.[44]

PROFILE OF HIGH TECH CEO

ATTENTION	Investigating	15%	(Moderate)
	Exploring	24%	(High)
INTENTION	Determining	3%	(Very Low)
	Evaluating	9%	(Low)
COMMITMENT	Timing	23%	(High)
	Anticipating	26%	(High)

These are dramatic, but not uncommon scenarios. Management teams that are allowed to coalesce through a process of natural selection tend to develop decision-making biases. A team of like-minded individuals can be very cohesive. It is not difficult to get a group of Attention-oriented managers to agree that matters really need more consideration. A group of strongly Intention-oriented individuals reinforce each other's sense that a position must be established and resolutely held with conviction. A group of Committers feed off each other's urge to just get on with it. But such cohesion can also result in groupthink, as the cautionary tales in this section illustrate.

Team Balance
If a senior team is to be successful over time, it must avoid the kinds of mistakes that arise from groupthink. In order to do so, in Lamb's view, the team

must be made up of people who take different types of initiatives. That is, team members need to have distinctively different action motivations. In this way, Investigating, Exploring, Determining, Evaluating, Timing, and Anticipating are all covered and no aspect of the decision-making process is overlooked.

Teams composed of people who make decisions in different ways are not without conflict. Managers who are high in Timing and Anticipating hate being slowed down by their more Attention- and Intention-oriented colleagues. Executives who are strongly motivated to Determine and Evaluate are inclined to see the information and ideas contributed by Attention-oriented colleagues as irrelevant, for they have already made up their minds. Attention-oriented individuals dislike being rushed into action without sufficient preparation and this can lead to conflict with Commitment-oriented coworkers. Those high in Investigating and Exploring may find their Intention-oriented colleagues judgmental, feeling that they form conclusions before all the facts are in. There are all sorts of ways that people with different decision-making styles can rub each other the wrong way. And yet, this is a necessary friction. When Movement Pattern Analysis is used to select, promote, and place managers, this is always done not only with an eye to matching the pattern of initiatives to job responsibilities, but also with a view to enhancing the decision-making balance of the team in which the manager will function.

For example, Lamb encountered a case of "like hires like" in a privately owned confectionary company. The top team, which consisted of the two owners and a sales manager, were all Attention-oriented. Thus, Lamb found that a lot of energy was being concentrated on preliminary consideration and planning, yet little was done to actualize plans. The consequences of this approach were demonstrated dramatically. The confectioners had been involved for several months in negotiations to purchase another company. Many congenial meetings had been held with the owners of the other enterprise and arrangements for purchase were being outlined with all due attention and care. On the basis of this thorough groundwork, the confectioners fully expected the acquisition to go through in due course. Consequently, they were dumbfounded to read in the morning paper one day that the company they wished to purchase had been bought by a competitor. After months of painstaking consideration, another group who were faster off the mark had gotten the prize![45]

Some time later, the Attention-oriented sales manager left the company. This provided Lamb with an opportunity to find a new sales manager whose preferred initiatives would complement the Attention-orientation of the co-owners. A suitable candidate was found, and, hoping for the best, Lamb introduced this Commitment-oriented manager into the team (see profiles below).

PROFILES OF TOP TEAM/CONFECTIONERS

		Co-Owner	Co-Owner	Sales Manager
ATTENTION	Investigating	Low	High	Low
	Exploring	High	High	Moderate
INTENTION	Determining	Low	High	Moderate
	Evaluating	High	Low	Low
COMMITMENT	Timing	Low	Moderate	High
	Anticipating	Moderate	Low	High

However, after only a few months on the job, the sales manager was ready to resign. "No one takes any action," he complained to Lamb. But Lamb persuaded the man to stay, and by gradual increments, his Commitment-oriented initiatives began to have impact. The new sales manager found he could capitalize on the solid groundwork laid by his Attention-oriented colleagues. They, in turn, came to appreciate his readiness to keep things moving along. The kind of inaction that had caused them to miss opportunities, as in the case of the acquisition, ceased occurring.

As Ramsden points out, well-balanced executive teams are made up of individuals who "complement rather than duplicate"[46] each other in action. While these teams are lively and dynamic, they are "far from friction free," for "the action motivations within individuals are like tensions pulling in different directions."[47] In her view, the action that arises as the result of these tensions will be effective action "because it is born out of a variety of influences."[48]

The Need for Awareness
In order for the tensions that arise when individuals make decisions in different

ways to result in effective action, it is necessary to foster awareness of decision-making style, both at the individual and team level. This is done through individual counseling as well as work with the team as a whole.

For example, the chart below reflects individual profiles of the seven-member management team of a UK-based manufacturing company. The team profile, derived by averaging each of the six action initiatives, is shown in the far right column. This reflects a potential for balanced action and decision making, especially as each of the six action motivations are represented by a team member with strength in that area of at least 20 percent. The key to realizing this potential lies in making individual members aware of each other's strengths, so that the potential for complementing is utilized. In his report to the managing director, the consultant highlighted these individual strengths. For example, he recommended relying on the Materials, Finance, and Engineering heads "when it is important to discriminate on points of detail."[49] This advice points to their shared emphasis on Investigating. The Engineering head (strong Exploring) should be used "when new thinking is needed to solve a problem." The Personnel and Manufacturing managers (strong Determining) can be counted on "to inject a sense of purpose and direction, particularly during difficult times," while

MANUFACTURING TEAM PROFILE		Managing Director	Materials Manager	Personnel Manager	Finance Manager	Sales/Marketing Manager	Chief Engineer	Manufacturing Manager	Team Average
ATTENTION	**Investigating**	15	22	14	22	18	21	16	18
	Exploring	10	16	7	13	7	29	5	12
INTENTION	**Determining**	10	10	20	13	16	10	21	14
	Evaluating	20	12	13	5	17	12	15	14
COMMITMENT	**Timing**	25	28	23	29	26	13	13	23
	Anticipating	20	12	23	18	16	15	30	19

the managing director's strong Evaluating can "ensure that the key issues are being identified and tackled realistically." The team already has a "built-in sense of urgency" (five members who are strong in Timing) and an awareness "of long-term considerations" (three members who are strong in Anticipating). This emphasis on Commitment may incline the team to "move ahead too quickly before all the groundwork has been laid." Counteracting this inclination is where awareness becomes vital.

Companies have been able to cultivate such awareness through regular review and discussion of Movement Pattern Analysis profiles. In Trebor Ltd., for example, MPA was utilized for nearly three decades. Ian Marks, managing director, reported that: "Executives are willing to talk to each other about their profiles without fear that this might cause them to lose out in any 'political' or 'rat race' type of internal struggle."[50]

Enrico Luigi Colavito, managing director of CIGA Hotels, had a similar experience. Following individual counseling, senior executives "recognized the validity of the work and accepted the truth of their profiles."[51] These profiles were then shared throughout the group. As a result, Colavito reported that managers "have a better understanding of each other's motivations. This has led to improved co-operation."[52]

Another case in point is Albany International, where Lamb advised on hiring, setting up management teams, and restructuring existing teams for over twenty-five years. Movement Pattern Analysis first came to the attention of Frank McKone, former president and CEO, when McKone was looking for tools to assist managers in working together effectively.

"I had done a lot of reading on management skills and attributes and how teams work together," McKone recalled. "I thought there must be some way to put all this information together in a manner that is logical and can be understood and followed up on. Lamb's work came to my attention."

"I can't defend the idea that motion study is the only element. But the resulting structure that Lamb gives is very helpful. He has a way of displaying his judgment on basic initiatives that explains six steps in the execution of plans. This is easy to understand and to explain to an individual."

"When you first get your profile, you don't anticipate your low areas. You think you are stronger in those areas. But when you look at the whole profile and the fact that there are other elements included, you realize, looking back, perhaps this is always where I have had very strong strengths and the low areas are where I get the assistance of other people. When you come to grips with that in your whole personality and outlook, it's fine. You can see the strength and advantages of having complementary people and how you can leverage on that."

"This is carried further in interaction charts, which allow you to see what happens when these individual traits come together in a team. Albany tends to keep people a long time, but we move them around a lot. When you introduce new people, it is good to know where they fit in. People have been making judgment calls on this in a less orderly way. We found this approach worked out quite well for the most part."[53]

Managers may remain disinterested or even skeptical that decision making can be assessed through movement analysis. But many find the resulting insight into key staff members to be of value. "You know all your friends and associates have different traits," observed one former CEO. "MPA just puts it down in a numerical and graphic form. This makes it faster and easier to understand."[54] D. I. Worthington, managing director of CCL Systems Limited, concurred, noting that the use of MPA had enabled his firm to be "far more objective in assessing the strengths and weaknesses of our management team."[55] Another client made a similar observation, noting that Movement Patttern Analysis "provides a frame of reference that allows understanding without judgment."[56]

Other MPA users have commented on its value for developing individuals and teams. P. C. Boon, managing director of Hoover, found that Movement Pattern Analysis gave him "a much wider perspective concerning the use of a manager's ability and, perhaps more importantly, a greater insight into achieving understanding and spontaneous cooperation within the management team."[57] George Greener, general manager, Mars BV, agreed: "I have found the techniques to be uniquely beneficial in the development of both teams and individuals."[58] As Professor Sir James Ball, former principal of the London Business School, sums up, "It is not always easy to see oneself in context, and an increasing awareness must be an important element in improving management capability."[59]

The Body-Mind Connection in the Workplace

Over the past 100 years, movement study has been utilized in the workplace in a number of different ways. In the early twentieth century, Taylor and the Gilbreths demonstrated that time and motion could be dissected to improve productivity and to enhance the ease and efficiency of manual labor. In the

1940s, Rudolf Laban introduced more motion factors into the analysis of work action, an innovation that made it possible to capture individual details of work movements with much greater refinement.

The initial industrial studies undertaken by Laban and F. C. Lawrence on this basis demonstrated the relationship between movement rhythm and efficiency, prevention of fatigue, and job satisfaction. More significantly, Laban and Lawrence recognized that movement rhythm underlies all human endeavor. This insight set the stage for the study of managerial function through the analysis of movement. This study was carried forward by Laban's protégé, Warren Lamb, in the 1950s. Through Lamb's painstaking research, detailed patterns of movement were matched to a framework of management initiative. The result, known as Movement Pattern Analysis, is an objective, idiographic representation of how an individual characteristically navigates through the decision-making process. As the case studies in this chapter have illustrated, awareness of these patterns of embodied initiatives has profound implications for individual careers, group decision-making responsibilities, and company performance.

As Professor Ball noted, increasing awareness is an important element in improving management capability. And, according to educator Moshe Feldenkrais, movement is the very basis of self awareness. "Most of what goes on within us remains dulled and hidden from us until it reaches the muscles," Feldenkrais explains. But, "We know what is happening within us as soon as the muscles of our face, heart, or breathing apparatus organize themselves into patterns."[60] Philosopher Thomas Hanna has referred to this internal, somatic awareness as a "unified experience of self-sensing and self-moving."[61] Since the sensory-motor system that governs voluntary action functions as a "closed-loop feedback system . . . we cannot sense without acting and we cannot act without sensing."[62]

Somatic practitioner Deane Juhan expresses the relationship of movement and awareness in this way:

> There is a mental feeling of "rightness" that comes to be associated with the specific manner of movement which produces satisfactory results. This sense of "rightness" is a large part of the pleasure of learning a skill, and is also one of the main reasons why habits become so ingrained, why my behavior takes on such recognizable personal patterns. So much of my sense of psychological and physical continuity, my sense of unity and

security, depends upon my ability to repeat appropriate and predictable actions, that this feeling of "rightness" can scarcely be overestimated in its importance as an element of my psychic integration as a whole.[63]

The psychologists Gordon Allport and Philip Vernon concur:

From our results it appears that a man's movements reflect an essentially stable and constant individual style. His expressive activities seem not to be dissociated and unrelated to one another, but rather to be organized and well-patterned. Furthermore, the evidence indicates that there is congruence between expressive movement and the attitudes, traits, values and other dispositions of the 'inner' personality.[64]

While thousands of individuals and hundreds of companies have utilized movement analysis, public recognition of the patterned nature of movement behavior and its congruence with the "inner" personality is still nascent. Perhaps we are not yet ready, as Olive Moore advocated at the outset of this chapter, to "think of human movement as we should—*as the outward and visible symbol of man entire.*"[65] Nevertheless, points of view from many different fields are converging on the relationship between body and mind and the implications of this relationship in the workplace. This renewed interest in the "bodily perspective" is encouraging and suggests that movement analysis will continue to provide insight into behavior from the factory floor to the executive suite. For, as Laban notes:

Although in analysis we look at movement from the standpoint of an outside observer, we should try to feel it sympathetically from within. A mind trained to assist bodily perspective, instead of combating it, would give us a completely new outlook on movement and therefore on life.[66]

Endnotes

1. Olive Moore, "Man of the Month: Rudolf Laban," *Scope: Magazine for Industry* (October 1954), 61.

2. The idiographic approach has been most prominently advocated by Gordon W. Allport and George W. Kelly and applied in the construction of, respectively, the Allport-Vernon-Lindzey Study of Values and the Role

Construct Repertory Test.

3. Frank McKone, interview with author, August 29, 2003.

4. Alan Devereux, quoted in Jules Arbose, "Movements Reveal Corporate Misfits," *International Management* (March 1979), 25.

5. Ibid.

6. Alan Devereux, memo to Pamela Ramsden, Warren Lamb Associates, June 29, 1976.

7. Ian Marks, quoted in Arbose, "Movements Reveal," 25.

8. The job specifications cited in the Arbose article were abridged. For more inclusive examples of the types of job specifications that were prepared, see Warren Lamb, *Posture and Gesture* (London: Gerald Duckworth, 1965), 156–173, and Warren Lamb and David Turner, *Management Behaviour* (London: Gerald Duckworth, 1969), 106–128.

9. Marks, quoted in Arbose, "Movements Reveal," 22.

10. This case was cited in "Square Pegs for Square Holes," *The Director* (June 1977).

11. Pamela Ramsden, quoted in Arbose, "Movements Reveal," 24.

12. Ibid.

13. Lamb, *Posture and Gesture*, 154.

14. Robert Jones, "Experience of an Advertising Man," *The Times* (February 14, 1972).

15. Ibid.

16. Ibid.

17. Ronald Meachen, interview with the author, June 18, 2003.

18. Warren Lamb, files on his work with Meachen, January 10, 1958.

19. Ibid.

20. Lamb, Meachen files, circa 1957.

21. Lamb, *Posture and Gesture*, 174.

22. Ibid, 183.

23. Meachen, interview.

24. Ibid.

25. Lamb, *Posture and Gesture*, 154.

26. Pamela Ramsden, *Top Team Planning* (London: Associated Business Programmes, 1973), 237.

27. Ibid.

28. Ibid.

29. Ibid.

30. Ibid.

31. Ibid.

32. Ibid.

33. The term *groupthink* was coined by psychologists Janis and Mann (1977) to delineate faulty decision-making processes that occur when conformity pressures prejudice the judgment of a group. Characteristics of groupthink are outlined in Michael Argyle, *The Psychology of Interpersonal*

Behaviour (London: Penguin, 1994).

34. Eden Davies, *Beyond Dance* (London: Brechin Books, 2001), 105.

35. Ibid., 107.

36. Ibid.

37. Ibid.

38. Ibid.

39. Warren Lamb, "Motivating by Strategy," *Management Today* (March 1984).

40. Ibid.

41. Ibid.

42. Ibid.

43. Ibid.

44. Warren Lamb, interview with author, June 11, 2003.

45. Ibid.

46. Pamela Ramsden, "The Power of Individual Motivation in Management," *Journal of General Management* (Winter 1975), 66.

47. Ibid.

48. Ibid.

49. Edward J. Bows, team report, April 24, 1988; all subsequent quotations are from this source.

50. Marks, quoted in Arbose, "Movements Reveal," 25.

51. Enrico Luigi Colavito, quoted in Arbose, "Movements Reveal," 25.

52. Ibid.

53. McKone, interview.

54. Ibid.

55. D. I. Worthington, quoted in Warren Lamb Inc. promotional materials, 1990.

56. This quotation is taken from evaluation materials compiled by MPA consultant Charlotte Honda, following a team-building exercise with administrators in the College of Fine Arts, Ohio University, 1988.

57. P. C. Boon, quoted in "Hoover Spring-cleans an Executive Suite," *Business Administration*, September 1973: 47.

58. George Greener, quoted in Warren Lamb Inc. promotional materials.

59. Professor James Ball, quoted in Warren Lamb Inc. promotional materials.

60. Moshe Feldenkrais, *Awareness through Movement* (New York: Harper & Row, 1972), 36.

61. Thomas Hanna, "What Is Somatics?" 341–352 in *Bone, Breath, & Gesture*, ed. Don Hanlon Johnson (Berkeley, CA: North Atlantic Books, 1995), 346.

62. Ibid., 345.

63. Deane Juhan, "Job's Body (excerpts)," 355–378 in *Bone, Breath, & Gesture*, ed. Don Hanlon Johnson (Berkeley, CA: North Atlantic Books, 1995), 372.

64. Gordon Allport and Philip Vernon, *Studies in Expressive Movement* (New York: Macmillan, 1933), 248.

65. Moore, "Man of the Month."

66. Rudolf Laban, *The Language of Movement* (Boston: Plays Inc., 1974), 90.

Selected Bibliography

Selected sources on work study, movement analysis, and the use of photography in movement study are listed. For the convenience of readers, the list has been divided into three categories of materials. Major books and articles are listed below, but interviews, newsletters, and other "fugitive" sources referred to in chapter endnotes are not repeated. Information on the unpublished archival materials utilized in the writing of this book will be found under a separate heading. Finally, for those who wish to pursue the subject of Movement Pattern Analysis further, various electronic sources are noted at the end.

Books and Articles

Allison, Nancy, ed. *The Illustrated Encyclopedia of Body-Mind Disciplines*. New York: Rosen, 1999.

Allport, Gordon, and Philip Vernon. *Studies in Expressive Movement*. New York: Macmillan, 1933.

Arbose, Jules. "Movements Reveal Corporate Misfits," *International Management* (March 1979): 22–25.

Argyle, Michael. *The Psychology of Interpersonal Behaviour*. London: Penguin, 1994.

Axtell, Robert. *Gestures*. New York: John Wiley & Sons, 1991.

Bartenieff, Irmgard, with Dori Lewis. *Body Movement: Coping with the Environment*. New York: Gordon and Breach, 1980.

Bergson, Henri. *The Creative Mind*. New York: Wisdom Library, 1946.

Blum, Milton L. *Industrial Psychology and Its Social Foundation*. New York: Harper and Brothers, 1949.

Brown, J.A.C. "The Social Psychology of Industry." In *Management and Motivation*, edited by Victor Vroom and Edward Deci. Harmondsworth, England: Penguin Books, 1970.

Damasio, Antonio. *Descartes' Error*. London: Papermac, 1996.

_____. *The Feeling of What Happens*. London: Vintage, 2000.

Daval, Jean-Luc. *Photography: History of an Art*. New York: Rizzoli, 1982.

Davies, Eden. *Beyond Dance: Laban's Legacy of Movement Analysis*. London: Brechin Books, 2001.

Davis, Flora. *Inside Intuition*. New York: New American Library, 1975.

Ekman, Paul. *Telling Lies*. New York: W. W. Norton, 1985.

Farr, James R. *World Eras: Industrial Revolutions in Europe 1750–1914*. Detroit: Thomson Gale, 2003.

Fast, Julius. *Body Language*. New York: Pocket Books, 1977.

Feldenkrais, Moshe. *Awareness through Movement*. New York: Harper & Row, 1972.

Frizot, Michel, ed. *A New History of Photography*. Cologne, Germany: Konemann, 1998.

Gardner, Howard. *Frames of Mind*. New York: Basic Books, 1985.

Gendlin, Eugene. *Focusing*. New York: Everest House, 1978.

Gilbreth, Frank B. Jr., and Ernestine Gilbreth Carey. *Cheaper by the Dozen*. New York: Wheeler Books, 1948.

Glaser, Barney, and Anselm Strauss. *The Discovery of Grounded*

Theory. Chicago: Aldine, 1967.

Goffmann, Erving. *The Presentation of Self in Everyday Life*. Garden City, NY: Doubleday, 1959.

Goldberg, Vicki, and Robert Silberman, *American Photography: A Century of Images*. San Francisco: Chronicle Books, 1999.

Hanna, Thomas. "What Is Somatics?" In *Bone, Breath, & Gesture*, edited by Don Hanlon Johnson. Berkeley, CA: North Atlantic Books, 1995.

Johnson, Mark. *The Body in the Mind*. Chicago: University of Chicago Press, 1987.

Jones, Robert. "Experience of an Advertising Man." *The Times*, February 14, 1972.

Juhan, Deane. "Job's Body (excerpts)." In *Bone, Breath, & Gesture*, edited by Don Hanlon Johnson. Berkeley, CA: North Atlantic Books, 1995.

Kestenberg, Judith. *Children and Parents: Psychoanalytic Studies in Development*. New York: Jason Aronson, 1975.

Kestenberg, Judith, and Mark Sossin. *The Role of Movement Patterns in Development*. New York: Dance Notation Bureau Press, 1979.

Laban, Rudolf, and F. C. Lawrence. *Effort*. London: MacDonald & Evans, 1947.

Laban, Rudolf. "What Has Led You to Study Movement?" *Laban Art of Movement Guild News Sheet*, No. 7 (September 1951): reprint/n.p.

_____. *The Language of Movement*. Boston: Plays Inc., 1974.

_____. *The Mastery of Movement*. Boston: Plays Inc., 1975.

_____. *A Life for Dance*. Translated by Lisa Ullmann. New York: Theatre Arts Books, 1975.

Lakoff, George, and Mark Johnson. *Philosophy in the Flesh*. New York: Basic Books, 1999.

Lamb, Warren. *Posture and Gesture*. London: Gerald Duckworth , 1965.

Lamb, Warren, and David Turner. *Management Behaviour*. London: Gerald Duckworth, 1969.

Lamb, Warren, and Elizabeth Watson. *Body Code*. London: Routledge & Kegan Paul, 1979.

Lamb, Warren. "Motivating by Strategy," *Management Today* (March 1984): reprint/n.p.

Lawrence, F. C. *Laban Art of Movement Guild Magazine* (December 1954): 26–27.

Masur, Gerhard. *Prophets of Yesterday*. New York: Macmillan, 1961.

Moore, Carol-Lynne. *Executives in Action*. London: Pitman, 1982.

Moore, Olive. "Man of the Month." *Scope Magazine for Industry* (October 1954): 60–72.

Morris, Desmond. *Manwatching*. New York: Harry Abrams, 1977.

Newhall, Beaumont. *The History of Photography*. New York: New York Graphic Society Books, 1982.

Peters, Alan. "Hoover Spring Cleans an Executive Suite," *Business Administration* (September 1973): 47–49.

Pierce, Alexandra, and Roger Pierce. *Expressive Movement*. New York: Plenum Press, 1989.

Preston-Dunlop, Valerie. *Rudolf Laban: An Extraordinary Life*. London: Dance Books, 1998.

Rabinbach, Anson. *The Human Motor*. Berkeley, CA: University of California Press, 1992.

Ramsden, Pamela. *Top Team Planning*. London: Associated Business Programmes, 1973.

Ramsden, Pamela. "The Power of Individual Motivation in Management," *Journal of General Management*, Vol. 3, No. 3 (Winter 1975/76): 52-66.

Rosenthal, Robert, Judith A. Hall, M. Robin DiMatteo, Peter L. Rogers, and Dane Archer. *Sensitivity to Nonverbal Communication*. Baltimore: Johns Hopkins Press, 1979.

Scheflen, Albert. *Body Language and Social Order*. Englewood Cliffs, NJ: Prentice-Hall, 1972.

Shawn, Ted. *Every Little Movement*. Brooklyn, NY: Dance Horizons, 1974.

"Square Pegs for Square Holes." *The Director* (June 1977): 29–30.

Stearns, Peter N., and John H. Hinshaw. *The ABC-CLIO World History Companion to the Industrial Revolution*. Santa Barbara, CA: ABC-CLIO, 1996.

Taylor, Frederick Winslow. "Scientific Management." In *Organizational Theory*, edited by D. S. Pugh. Harmondsworth, England: Penguin Books, 1971.

Todd, Mabel Ellsworth. *The Thinking Body*, Brooklyn, NY: Dance Horizons, 1973.

Wainwright, Gordon R. *Body Language*. London: Hodder & Stoughton, 2003.

Welton, Donn, ed. *The Body*. Oxford: Blackwell, 1999.

Willson, F. M. G. *In Just Order Move: The Progress of the Laban Centre for Movement and Dance, 1946-1996*. London: Athlone Press, 1996.

Wolfgang, Aaron. *Everybody's Guide to People Watching*. Yarmouth, ME: Intercultural Press, 1995.

Archival Sources

The National Resource Centre for Dance (NRCD), based at the University of Surrey, in Guildford, England, is the primary repository for the Rudolf Laban Archive and the Warren Lamb Archive. The Laban Archive, which contains papers from the final two decades of Laban's career in England, is a vast collection with a great deal of material on the application of movement analysis in industry. The Lamb Archive contains material that chronicles Lamb's consulting career and the development of Movement Pattern Analysis, complementing the material in the Laban Archive. Members of the public may visit the NRCD to undertake research. Appointments must be booked in advance and there is a modest fee for use. More information on the archive collections is available on the website: www.surrey.ac.uk/NRCD.

Web Sites

http://www.motushumanus.org—This site gives information on training and professional standards.

http://www.brechinpublishing.co.uk—This is a source for books, articles, and a bibliography dealing with movement study.

http://www.movementpatternanalysis.net—This provides general infomation on MPA.

INDEX

M

machines, 1, 10, 15
making a commitment, 42, 44,
    48, 79, 82
management, 10, 12, 16, 40, 42,
    50–51, 91, 96, 106
manufacturing, 4–5, 30–31, 104,
    109
Marey, Etienne-Jules, 7–9, 14
Marks, Ian, 98, 110
Mars Company, 27, 36, 111
Martin, Christopher, 20
mass production, 1, 29
Masur, Gerhard, 10
Mayo, Elton, 16
McKone, Frank, vi, 110
Meachen, Ronald, vi, 100–101
means of production, 5
mechanization of labor, 4
mobile phrases of bodily action,
    65
mood, 37, 60, 66–72
Moore, Olive, 96, 113
motion factors, 58–59, 72, 112
motivation, 42, 86, 88, 92–93,
    103, 107–110
movement dynamism, 70
movement harmony, 69–70, 86
movement observation
    procedures, 38
Movement Pattern Analysis, vi,
    37, 47, 51, 86, 98, 100,
    102–103, 107, 110–112
Muybridge, Eadweard, 6–8

N

neutral style, 48, 89

Nobunaga, 2
notation, 20–24, 32, 39

O

observational methodology, 32
occupations, 2, 4–5
Osborne Group, 99–100
output, 6, 10–13, 16, 24, 28

P

pace, 5, 44, 58–59, 68, 72, 82,
    94
Park, Robert, 64
Paton Lawrence & Co., 26–27,
    36, 38
pattern of action, 1–3, 44, 102
perspective, 41–42, 44–46, 60,
    81–82, 86, 89–90, 94, 111,
    113
photographic gun, 8
Pierce, Alexandra and Roger, 56,
    60
planar scheme, 61
planes, horizontal, vertical,
    sagittal, 61–62, 64, 68, 71,
    73, 81–82, 85–86, 91, 101
Posture and Gesture, 39, 41, 99,
    102
precision, 6–7, 25, 28
precision with flow effort, 40
preindustrial, 4–5, 16
Preston-Dunlop, Valerie, 28
private style, 48, 88
productivity, 2, 4–6, 10, 12–14,
    16, 24, 28, 30–31, 111

R

Rabinbach, Anson, 9–10
Ramsden, Pamela, 51, 99, 102, 108
reassignment, 30, 36
relaxation, 24, 26, 28
resisting, 16, 59
retreating, 62, 73, 82, 86–88
rhythm, vi, 22–32, 36–38, 40, 42, 112
risk, 44, 82, 103, 105
rising, 62, 64, 68, 71, 73, 82, 87, 88
Rodin, Auguste, 7, 63

S

Sansome, Arthur, 98
Scheflen, Albert, 64
Scientific Management, 10, 12, 16
Scotcros Ltd., 97
second form, 60–62
second industrial revolution, 4
selection, 2–3, 31, 47, 97, 106
shadow movements, 38
shape, 8, 40–41, 60–64, 66, 68, 70–73, 79, 81–83, 85–86, 88–92, 100, 101
shape dynamism, 70
sharing style, 50, 86
Shawn, Ted, 60
shogun, 2
space factor, 58
spatial design, 22, 40
specialization, 4–5
spreading, 62, 64, 72, 81, 87–88, 90

stable arrangements of the body, 65
Stanford, Leland, 6
Stearns, Peter, 5
Stevens, Peter, 71, 73

T

Taylor, Frederick Winslow, 10–14, 16, 24, 28, 31, 97, 111
team analysis, 102–103
teamwork, 30–31
temporal graphs of motion, 8
Therblig, 13, 23, 32
time and motion studies, 97
time factor, 58
Timing, 24, 44, 79, 82, 92, 94, 98, 100–101, 103, 105, 107, 110
Todd, Mabel Ellsworth, 56, 63, 86
trace-forms, 61–63, 73, 85
trait and factor theory, 26, 47
transitory, 65–67, 73
Trebor Ltd., 98, 110
Turner, Bryan, 1
Turner, David, 71
Tyresoles, 25–26

V

Vernon, Philip, 113
versatile style, 50, 90
vertical orientation, 41
vertical plane, 61–62, 64, 68, 73, 82, 85, 101
vocations, 5
voluntary motions, 56